A Century of Service

A Century of Service

An illustrated history of the
National Union of Public Employees

1889-1993

Bob Fryer and Steve Williams

Lawrence & Wishart
London

Lawrence & Wishart Ltd
144a Old South Lambeth Road
London SW8 1XX

First published in 1993
Text copyright © Bob Fryer and Steve Williams

ISBN 0 85315 792 8

Cover and text design by Jan Brown Designs
Printing and binding by John Goodman, Birmingham.

Thanks to Peter Farquharson, retired NUPE area officer, for the loan of badges for the cover illustration.

Contents

NUPE has become a major union. We've built up our membership, taken part in major disputes, brought women to the fore and democratised our structure. We've campaigned for better and more responsive public services; and resisted privatisation. We've won political support for a national minimum wage; and tackled unequal pay.

It is a proud history. We have a union with good local organisation and effective leadership, able to work in unity with other organisations. But in the 100 years of our existence, we have scarcely faced more difficult times than today.

Ina Love, President of NUPE, to the National Conference, May 1989

Foreword

This illustrated history of NUPE has been produced just a few weeks before the union comes to an end. From July 1993 the members of NUPE, NALGO and COHSE will form a new public services union, to be called UNISON. At its foundation this new amalgamated union will be the largest in the UK, and one of the biggest in Europe. It will represent more women workers than any other union in this country and more part-timers. After more than a century of constant striving for the better organisation of public service workers, the new union represents an outstanding achievement for NUPE and its partners.

For generations, the men and women who built up NUPE dreamed of creating a single, powerful trade union for workers in the public services. From their origins amongst the Vestry employees in London, NUPE's public service workers have struggled both to improve pay and conditions and to defend the provision of the services themselves. For generations, they have fought off the profiteering of private contractors and the attempts of employers to oppress the workers. NUPE's members and officers know only too well that the self-same struggles are continuing today. Attempts to put the clock back are still being valiantly resisted by NUPE.

The record set out in the words and pictures of this commemorative book is a very proud one for our union. From only small beginnings amongst road sweepers, sewage workers, and institutional workers, NUPE eventually grew to number over 700,000 members in the early 1980s. This achievement rested on the untiring efforts of tens of thousands of low paid men and women, often risking their own jobs in order to organise and represent their fellow workers.

It took NUPE's organisers into the country lanes and highways to recruit the county roadmen, ignored by other unions. They went into schools, hospitals and social services to recruit the thousands of part-time women workers who had been largely ignored by other unions. It meant facing the opposition both of the employers and of the general unions. It meant campaigning for recognition, for seats on negotiating bodies and for the establishment of national rates of pay and conditions. It also meant fighting low pay and calling for support for its policies from other unions, the TUC and the Labour Party.

For over a century, NUPE's members have served the public in this country. Similarly, thousands of NUPE's branch officials and the union's officers have striven to serve our members. They have done so in a union typified by friendship and closeness, determined to fight poverty and unfairness wherever they are encountered. It is a culture we are honoured to carry forward into UNISON: it is one we are proud to record in this commemorative volume.

Rodney Bickerstaffe
General Secretary

Anna McGonigle
President

1. Beginning to organise
1889-94

THE GROWTH OF MUNICIPAL SERVICES

During the nineteenth century, society underwent a radical transformation. Manufacturing replaced agriculture as the prime source of wealth, creating a process which drew workers away from the land and into the emerging towns and cities.

The living and working conditions in these new urban areas quickly became the subject of concern and local authorities were forced by legislation to improve standards of public health.

Some authorities established effective and wide ranging municipal services, engendering a sense of civic pride and achievement. For these progressive bodies, developments such as gas, electricity and tramways were seen as opportunities for exercising public control through municipal enterprise.

Other local authorities were less ambitious, providing only the statutory minimum of services, believing their duty to the rate-payer to be paramount. This parsimony inevitably had its effect on the wages and conditions of local authority employees. Road-sweepers, dustmen, and road and sewer workers were among the lowest paid manual workers in the third quarter of the century. A survey of these grades in 1886 found that more than 80 per cent earned less than twenty-five shillings a week average. The lowest pay was reserved for the rural areas where the survey noted 'rates of wages are largely governed by rates of wages paid in the same neighbourhood to agricultural labourers'.

Wages in London, although generally higher than for the rest of the country, were still very poor. Charles Booth's notable investigation in 1891 found nearly six out of ten municipal workers living on wages of between twenty and twenty-five shillings – a level on or near the poverty line.

Indeed the capital was in many ways behind the progressive and reforming authorities in the provinces, in that it had not undergone thorough-going local government reform, and this had held back progress in the field of public health. A number of these archaic public bodies still employed contractors to perform their duties, with inefficiency and corruption as inevitable consequences. Contractors were certainly among the worst employers of labour, squeezing wages in order to maximise profits.

LONDON BEGINNINGS

It was against this background that trade unionism emerged in municipal services. Encouraged by the successful action of the gas workers and dockers in the East End of London in the summer of 1889, municipal workers began to form their own trade unions.

The birthplace was the parish of Camberwell in South East London, where 400 manual workers were employed on average conditions for London. Carmen – horse and cart

William Alexander Coote, the 'father of the Vestry Employees Union'. As a member of the Camberwell Vestry he helped organise the workers and acted as Secretary and President of the union in its infancy. He also played a role in establishing the Municipal Officers Association, with the Camberwell Vestry Clerk, C.W. Tagg in 1893-4, which went on to become one of the constituent parts of NALGO in 1905.

Improving wages and conditions of London municipal employees was a difficult task because of the mentality of the elected members:

❛ … the London vestries seem to have been guided by a penny pinching, pound foolish philosophy. The first and often the sole question raised about a suggested improvement was the cost and such issues as superannuation allowances for officers about to retire produced pitched battles, in which the outlook of the small business man was at its most myopic. To some of them, apparently, nothing mattered but the rates, and the surest way to get elected was to make resounding attacks on the extravagance of old members and resounding promises to cut the rates.❜ D. Owen, *The Government of Victorian London*, 1982, p219

London road-menders enjoying a
dinner break, 1892.

John Cole, the first General
Secretary of the Vestry Employees
Union.

drivers – worked a sixty-five hour week for a
wage of twenty-four shillings, while road
sweepers worked fifty-eight and a half hours
for nineteen shillings. Both groups therefore
earned considerably less per hour than the
dockers who had just established an hourly
rate of sixpence.

These comparisons were undoubtedly
used at the first meeting of the Carmen and
Roadmen's Union of the Parish of Camberwell established in early October 1889.
Presided over by William Coote, a progressive
member of the elected authority – the Vestry
– the meeting drew up a claim to present to
the Vestrymen. It asked for an improvement
in pay and requested that the members take
into account that, 'We are out in all weathers,
in the heat and in the cold, and find the sum
we receive is not sufficient to provide us and
our families with the bare necessities of life.'
Conciliatory and respectful in tone, the claim
was presented to the members by Coote himself who emphasised that it did not foreshad-
ow anything in the way of a strike. Some
members accused Coote of 'pressing' the
men to sign the claim, but the meeting
agreed there was a case to be heard and the
matter was referred to a committee. When it
reported, improvements were made to
sweepers and gullymen's pay, but all other
groups were ignored.

The impact of the events in Camberwell
was, however, more important than the small
concessions won. The message that a union
for unskilled municipal workers had been
formed quickly spread across South London.
Workers in Lambeth, Borough and
Bermondsey joined up, forcing a change in
name in 1890 to the South London Vestry
Employees Labour Union.

William Coote took on the Secretary's job
while the union found its feet, but by the
middle of 1890 a permanent man had been
found in John Cole, a former Camberwell
sweeper, introduced at a subsequent meeting
as 'a late MP-mud-pusher'. Cole was soon at
work submitting claims to authorities where
the union had recruited members. Contact
was made with progressive Vestry members,
and meetings of 'rate-payers' organised, passing resolutions backing the employees'
claims. Letters were written to the local press
and public demonstrations held with prominent speakers, including on many occasions
John Burns, a leader of the dock strike and
by now a prominent member of the London
County Council (LCC), which was set up in
1889.

This public campaigning had the immediate effect of bringing the issue of municipal
employees' abysmal pay levels into the public
glare and a number of authorities reacted by

dismissing union activists. In one case the union was strong enough to turn the tables, as was reported to the *Workman's Times* by two correspondents, 'Dust and Slop', in 1892:

> ... go to Bermondsey and see how things work there. Two years ago the Secretary [of the Vestry Employees Union] was dismissed twice and re-instated by the Vestry against the wishes of the Superintendent. Now the table is turned and the Superintendent has gone and the Branch Secretary has taken his place and the old gang is completely smashed up. So, officials please beware.

Bermondsey, by 1890, had become a Progressive and Labour controlled Vestry, receptive to union demands that it should be a 'model employer'. Basic wages were increased to a minimum of twenty-nine shillings a week, a week's holiday was granted and a sick pay scheme established. A 'closed shop' was also introduced and a new disciplinary code set up, removing the right of the surveyor to dismiss employees with more than three months service.

The Vestry Employees Union had through their campaigning and agitation helped establish the new majority in Bermondsey, and the lesson was not lost on the organisation, adding to their growing conviction that, as municipal employees, they were in a unique position, being able to exert an influence over who their employers were. Local branches were advised to join election committees, secure commitments of support for vestry employees from candidates, and deliver the vote on polling day. This strategy helped boost the confidence of workers who previously were regarded as only one step away from the workhouse; now they could help shape local politics. 'Dust and Slop', again as correspondents to *Workman's Times*, captured this feeling well when they wrote of their union's policy of helping to 'turn out old fossils' at election time and 'returning men who are prepared to grapple with the labour question and get a Union rate of wages for all men employed, either directly or indirectly, by any public body'.

Cole himself was nominated to stand for the Vestry in Camberwell in 1891 and elected on the Liberal and Radical slate, after being commended for the position by the London evening newspaper *The Star* for his reforming qualities and 'first hand knowledge of the working of Vestrydom that few candidates possess'. The union's General Secretary now joined a small group of Vestry Employees Union members – some honorary – who sat on elected public authorities. Among these the best known, perhaps, was Will Steadman, who was a member of the LCC and the Mile End Vestry. The union contributed heavily to his wages fund, which, in the days before representatives were paid, enabled him to devote sufficient time to his important public duties. Steadman later went on to become President of the TUC and Member of Parliament. For his part, Steadman stuck with the union and its successors, consistently supporting the claims for improvements.

Such emphasis was placed on the electoral work of the Vestry Employees Union that it displaced another aspect of trade union organisation – the ability to strike. The union had no time for strikes, which were seen as counter-productive when the electoral weapon was on hand.

As Cole said in his evidence to the Royal Commission on Labour in 1892:

> Our organisation is established on the principle of avoiding strikes. Although we as an organisation do not believe in strikes, that is only as it relates to us, because we so shape our course that we obtain at Vestry elections what other organisations have to provide a strike fund for. We strike through the ballot box.

Success at election time was also mirrored in success on the recruiting field. New branches were established across the capital as the Vestry Employees Union began to be recognised as an emerging influence on the London scene. Significant groups of employees of the recently established LCC began to look to the union for assistance.

THE QUALIFICATION OF POOR-LAW GUARDIANS.

Mr. HURLEY (London) proposed :—

" That this Congress is of opinion that the property and rating qualification for seats on Boards of Guardians and Local Boards in England and Wales, of members of Parochial Boards in Scotland, and Poor-law Guardians in Ireland is an anomaly which ought no longer to exist, and hereby instructs the Parliamentary Committee to take steps to secure its speedy abolition."

A man should have an equal right to sit and vote on those boards whether he lived in a castle or a cabin. (Hear, hear.) This proposal they should strongly back up as representatives of labour, because those local boards were becoming, and would become more so in the future, large employers of labour. They should seek to get the present qualifications abolished in order that they might place men of their own class on those boards.

Mr. M'INTYRE (Glasgow) seconded the resolution. (Cries of " Agreed.")

Without further discussion, the resolution was passed.

Con Hurley, the Vestry Employees Union organiser, spoke at the 1892 TUC in favour of the abolition of property and rating qualifications for candidates in municipal elections. They were abolished in 1894.

Clearing the drains in Westminster, c 1895.

WESTMINSTER CITY COUNCIL LIBRARIES

ORGANISING THE LCC

The LCC had begun its work in amid enormous expectations of its ability to bring a new reforming zeal to London local government. It had a progressive majority, among them a number of well known trade union figures, who pushed through some worthwhile changes, including the fair wage clause which was written into all council contracts. The Council claimed to put the 'labour question' at the top of its list of priorities, but its actions often turned out to be at variance with its image.

Servants in the Council's asylums were one group who tried to win improvements, particularly a reduction in the excessive fourteen hour day. At first these demands were made by attendants and nurses independent of any union backing, but as they were repeatedly rejected by the Council, so they began to look for assistance to other groups of workers.

Manual workers employed by the Council in its 'main-drainage' work were organising into unions in the autumn of 1889 and submitting numerous claims. They were led by the men at the Northern Outfall works at Beckton, which was very close to the principal scene of activity during the gas workers' strike some months earlier. Not surprisingly, they joined the East Ham Branch of the Gas Worker's Union, which included its leading figure Will Thorne. Demands for an eight hour day, five shillings a day minimum, one week's annual holiday and an end to local dismissals were put to the Council in 1890, with the prospect of a strike if they were not met. Concessions were made to one group, the flushers, who got an eight hour shift, seven pence an hour and protective clothing.

Among the Northern Outfall employees was a young engine labourer by the name of Albin Taylor. He was born in Castle Cary in Somerset in 1866 and after only a minimum of education he ran away from home to work on the Severn Tunnel, which was then under construction. From there he joined the Royal Marines and served in Egypt in 1884, with the British Expeditionary Force, only to be invalided out of the service in October 1885.

Taylor came to London and worked as a labourer in the building industry before securing a more permanent job at Beckton. He moved to the Canning Town area and quickly absorbed himself into the socialist politics which was slowly emerging in this exclusively working-class community. Like Will Thorne, who also lived in the area, he joined the Marxist Social Democratic Federation, attended its meetings, read and sold its weekly newspaper *Justice* and took part in its agitation, particularly among the unemployed. By 1891 he was a prominent enough figure in local socialist politics to be selected by the Labour Election Committee in South West Ham to fight a seat in the Borough Council elections. Although Taylor was not elected, a number of labour candidates were, and the West Ham Council began to change complexion; within a few years it would have a socialist majority.

Taylor quickly became involved in the activity of the union at the Northern Outfall works, but he became dissatisfied with the management of the Gas Workers Union, claiming it was spending excessive amounts on administration while membership was falling. By October 1891 he had helped establish a branch of the Vestry Employees

---

WITH the object of advocating the payment of the trade union rate of wages to all municipal workers a demonstration took place on Sunday afternoon in Brockwell Park under the auspices of the Vestry Employés' Union. An imposing procession, with bands and banners, left St. George's Church, Borough, about two o'clock and proceeded to the park via Southwark Bridge-road, Kennington-road, Brixton-road, Water-lane, and along Dulwich-road. Upon arriving there a mass meeting was held, and when the proceedings commenced there must have been several thousand Vestry employés assembled round the brake in which the speakers were seated. The crowd included contingents representing the Whitechapel, Islington, Lambeth, Bermondsey, Rotherhithe, Camberwell, and Greenwich branches of the Union. There was also a strong body from the National Gas Workers' Union.

———

MR. J. HARDING (president of the Union) occupied the chair, and in his opening remarks complained that the Lambeth Vestry was far behind the others in the matter of wages, in fact he thought they were scarcely paid at all. MR. VINCENT moved the following resolution : " That this meeting considers that the scale of wages laid down by the National Municipal and Vestry Employés' Union is both reasonable and just, and pledges itself to do all in its power to induce the Vestries, the London County Council, and other public bodies to set an example to private enterprise by paying a living rate of wages, and working their men a reasonable number of hours." They were only asking for a reasonable wage. He knew the ratepayers would object, but he would remind them that they were now paying large salaries to officials for doing nothing.

Report of a Vestry Employees Union demonstration, London, 18 May 1983.

4 *A Century of Service*

March 13th 1893

A Special of the Branch was held at which Councillor Thorne & Bro. Hurley attended Councillor Thorne addressed the Branch promising them all the support he could give them as to the petition for better Wages etc Bro Goodyear then pro Bro Green he that a hearty vote of thanks be accorded Councillor Thorne for his attendance & his Address Bro Hurley then addressed the Meeting after which it was pro by Bro Green he by Bro Goodyear that a Special Meeting of the Branch be called for next Monday evening. & that 1000 handbills be printed for the Occasion. Carried Meeting Closed at 9:20

A. Taylor. Sec

Minutes of the West Ham branch of the Vestry Employees Union, 13 March 1893, showing Will Thorne in attendance. Albin Taylor remained secretary of the branch until October 1893.

Union at the Beckton Works, and was acting as its secretary. His involvement increased and by 1892 he was also secretary of a new branch in West Ham.

Just as LCC employees were joining the Vestry Employees Union in large numbers, so were other groups of municipal workers across London, so that by the end of 1891, membership had reached 3000. Clearly, the organisation had outgrown its South London base and at the annual meeting in March 1891, new rules were drafted to reflect these developments. The name was changed to the National Municipal and Incorporated Vestry Employees Labour Union – although members and others continued to refer to it as the Vestry Employees Union.

Included in the new rules was a six pounds funeral benefit on the death of a member – or three pounds on the death of a member's wife – a significant amount for the early 1890s, particularly on a membership contribution of two pence a week. This set the union apart from its main competitor, the Gas Workers Union, who under the militant leadership of Thorne had set themselves against such payments. Thorne argued that 'friendly' benefits detracted from the fighting spirit of unionism by offering palliatives instead of solutions. Municipal employees, however, saw the funeral benefit of the Vestry Employees Union as an important reason for joining. For them the prospect of a pauper burial was the ultimate indignity and if the union guaranteed that they could avoid it, as well as improving their wages and conditions,

they were very pleased at the extra benefit.

Without doubt, those members who worked for private contractors undertaking public work appreciated any benefit the union could bring to their lives. Their wages and conditions were among the very worst, as at Poplar and Limehouse, where dustmen were paid fifteen shillings for working a six day week, from half past five in the morning until nine o'clock at night. Contractors expected their employees to tout for tips and then would reduce the wage by the amount collected.

These and other abuses the union helped bring to the attention of the public, which by the early 1890s was becoming informed of cases of corruption and monopolistic practices by contractors. *The Star* newspaper commented on this in 1891:

The influence of the contractors is still very powerful in Vestry-dom. Some of the old abuses such as giving contracts to Vestry-men's relatives are stamped out, but there is not fair competition between the contractors. The public work given out by the vestries is practically in the hands of the monopolists. The contractors combine and arrange who is to have the job as soon as it is advertised.

Organisation of Municipal Labor.—The unfurling of the fine new silk banner of the Hackney branch of the National Municipal Vestry Employés Labor Union, by Alderman Fletcher Moulton, Q.C., M.P., was the occasion of a large and jubilant gathering of labor representatives at the Hackney Town-hall, on Monday evening. The worthy chairman of the Vestry, Mr. Charles Button, J.P., occupied the chair, supported by all sections of the Vestry, and the speakers also included the South Hackney councillors, Messrs. Smith and Humphreys. A hearty vote of thanks was passed to the labor party on the Vestry, who have secured, in a very short time, a minimum wage of 24s. a week for the Vestry employés, a week's holiday in the summer, trade union wages in all contracts, one o'clock closing instead of four on Saturdays, and many minor reforms; while the formation of a sick fund is in progress. In unfurling the banner, Mr. Moulton said the best mark of progress was the growth of sympathy between all classes, which had shown itself in London, and especially in Hackney, in two remarkable ways. In the first place, public bodies had grown to feel that they ought to be model employers of labor, and secondly, the servant of a public body must feel it a point of honor to give a fair day's work for a fair day's pay. Under such conditions work was done better and cheaper; and he felt certain that trade unions had been the means of substituting friendship and sympathy for suspicion and jealousy between employer and employed.

The unfurling of a union banner was always a great occasion, providing a symbol of the union's achievements, London, 23 May 1895.

Emblem of the National Municipal Labour Union.

ing, and it would not be long before direct labour could claim a full house.

Among the authorities who favoured direct labour were some who refused to recognise the union. They resented the intrusion of trade unions – often referred to as 'outsiders' – into the affairs of the vestry, and rebutted claims for improvements with statements of how they didn't need to be told how to treat their employees. Typical of this was the comment by a Whitechapel Vestryman, who in rejecting a union claim for an enhanced rate for bank holiday work said, 'the men would perhaps someday realise that the Board were their friends and not Mr Cole'. Some surveyors were also hostile to the union, especially when their once absolute power over the employees became challenged and elementary disciplinary procedures were established. They also disliked the ability of the union to push up wages and so increase the costs of providing the service. The Hackney surveyor complained of this in 1893, when he wrote, 'Labour Unions also seriously affect expenditure for labour. Workmen are urged to discontent and naturally unite in endeavour to obtain more wages and to work less hours for the higher pay.' Over in Hampstead, the attitude of the elected members to the union was shown when permission to use the vestry hall for a banner unfurling was rejected, and the stone-yard offered as an alternative.

Some of the worst areas for the Vestry Employees Union were in the wealthy West End of London. Paddington paid its sweepers eighteen shillings, while Westminster and Kensington paid twenty-one shillings – bringing them well within Charles Booth's definition of poverty wages. Women scrubbers employed by the Chelsea Board of Guardians were paid only nine shillings a week and, as a contemporary survey pointed out, a day's illness would be sufficient to force such workers to seek relief from the rates, 'and the Board

Important public figures, such as municipal engineers and surveyors, were also helping to shape local opinion against contracting out. Evidence of the greater efficiency, flexibility and control of directly employed labour emerged steadily from leading journals and opinion makers, helping to establish an unanswerable case. One by one the vestries set up their own operations and the influence of the contractors was squeezed out of London's affairs. By 1891 only one in eight vestries still employed contractors for sweep-

Municipal workers' trade unionism was undoubtedly inspired by the successes of other unskilled workers across London in 1889, as the General Secretary of the National Municipal Labour Union, John Fitch, later remarked:

❛ We are one of the many trade societies that sprang into existence with the great progressive movement that followed the Dock Strike. The docker had got his tanner, and we, as municipal employees, thought we were entitled to the same.❜ *London,* 4 March 1897

then finds itself rescuing from starvation its own underpaid work people.'

The irony of this was not lost on the union's general secretary, John Cole, who told the Royal Commission on Labour in 1892 that:

> We find that it is not the parishes that can afford to pay the high wages that do pay them. For instance, Bermondsey are paying the whole of their able bodied men, dustmen, carmen or whatever they are, 29/3. We find that the West End parishes do not pay more than 24 shillings.

Union pressure was kept up in these areas but little progress was made. The social class make-up of the constituencies guaranteed Moderate (Tory) majorities, and the elected members were not forced to accept the significance of the 'labour question'. Members inevitably became frustrated and this surfaced at a protest meeting in May 1893, when the Kensington union secretary, Joseph Bates, called the elected members 'the biggest set of blackguards and liars which it is possible to have.' But strong words were not enough to shift reactionary members, and in these authorities the union's policy of striking through the ballot box had a very hollow ring about it.

THE DEPARTURE OF JOHN COLE

Important though these bad employers were, they represented only pockets of failure in what was an overall picture of achievement for the union. John Cole spoke of this at the annual meeting in May 1893, when he claimed that the union had 'effected a wonderful change in the last three years', with nearly every authority in London making concessions to one group or another worth something like £30,000 a year to employees. Cole and his colleagues were optimistic about the future; equipped with the new demand of a thirty shilling minimum, they believed campaigning could be taken beyond the capital. The London membership of nearly 6000 – 60 per cent of all municipal employees – provided the base on which a further expan-

Watering and brushing the pavement in Clerkenwell, c 1900.
NATIONAL FILM AND PHOTOGRAPHIC LIBRARY

The early unions had some success in limiting the power of local authority officers to discipline workers at will, and gradually procedures were established giving the worker the opportunity for representation and appeal. However, the regime adopted by the employer could still vary considerably:

❛ Some believe that constant superintendence is essential for labour of every kind. While others strive to dispense with overlooking and endeavour to secure a response by other means: some employers try to touch men's hearts, others their fears; some look far ahead and, with abundant care, endeavour to train up and secure the services of a body of men who may become their trusted helpers, while others are content to meet the business necessity of the moment, and, guided mainly by the supply that offers of the particular labour they require, think little or nothing of people, but everything of results. ❜

C Booth, *Life and Labour of the People of London*, 1903, 2nd Series Vol 5, p215

When the London County Council was established in 1889, the Progressive Party won control, beating the Tory Moderates overwhelmingly. The Progressives have been described as a:

❛ … broad coalition of small businessmen and traders non-conformists and working-class radicals and enemies of the City monopolists. ❜

E J Hobsbawm, *Labour's Turning Point*, 1974, p132

Among these was the working-class socialist, John Burns, who was to be a close friend of municipal workers' trade unions. Seen here in 1885 holding a copy of the socialist newspaper *Justice.*

sion was to occur. Cole, however, did allude to a possible problem when he spoke of funeral benefits. These payments had been going up considerably, with many young men dying between the ages of twenty-five and twenty-nine years, imposing a severe strain on the union's finances. In a letter written in 1893 to one of the union's closest friends, John Burns, now socialist MP for Battersea, Cole referred to the 'great hinderance to our usefulness in funeral benefits… I know we cannot very well alter it at once, but I think in time we can, so that we can have the 2d. a week for our own work.'

If the union was running into financial problems in 1893, things were to get worse in early 1894, when John Cole inflicted a severe blow by absconding with union funds.

The temptation of having large sums of money available in cash was obviously too great for Cole and, like a number of other trade union general secretaries in the 1890s, his term of office ended in embezzlement. Common occurrence or not, the executive needed to move quickly to limit the damage and they did this by appointing John Fitch, a well known municipal employee from Greenwich. Fitch had been removed from the employment of the Greenwich vestry ostensibly on the ground that he was 'too well educated to sweep the streets', but the union activists alleged victimisation.

After Cole's departure, the union tried to carry on as if nothing had happened, but already groups of members were moving to divorce themselves from an organisation which inevitably had lost some credibility. A strong branch in Battersea, with more than 200 members, decided as a result of Cole's embezzlement to leave the union and establish their own organisation under the name of the Battersea Vestry Employees Labour Union.

Moving east along the River Thames, another well organised section of membership was also leading a breakaway from the Vestry Employees Union. Led by Albin Taylor at the Northern Outfall works, and sewer flusher William Anderson, from Bow, meetings of LCC employees were convened and support canvassed for a new union. It was duly established in April 1894, first as the London County Council Employees Labour Union and then, when it was necessary to register the rules, as the London County Council Employees Protection Association (LCCEPA). Taylor became organiser and Anderson General Secretary, both at this stage lay positions. The Executive was dominated by manual workers employed in the Council's main drainage service, although the President, J.S. Thomas of Sutton, and at least one other, came from the asylums sited on the fringe of the capital.

The arrival of the LCCEPA in the spring of 1894 provided unwelcome competition for the ailing Vestry Employees Union. Up to this point they had been given an almost free hand in organising municipal employees in London. Certainly the Gas Workers had made little impression across the metropolis, in contrast to their significant municipal membership in the provinces.

A self inflicted wound, which grew out of a fault line in the Vestry Employees Union's finances, had thrown open the field of organisation once again, and the next few years were to prove decisive in determining the shape of municipal workers unionism in its birthplace.

2. Dissent
1894-1907

THE NMLU

As if to give a new start for the Vestry Employees Union, the delegates present at the annual meeting in May 1894 agreed to simplify the title of the organisation to the National Municipal Labour Union (NMLU). Although membership had fallen by 20 per cent in a few months, the union was still an important influence in London's municipal affairs. General secretary John Fitch and his Executive Council were still optimistic about the future and within a few months had some successes which they could point to as evidence that the tide was turning in their favour.

In the vestry elections of November 1894, the Progressives gained control of five authorities and increased their majorities in three others. During the campaign the NMLU issued a programme of demands which local branches put to candidates to test opinions. It included a thirty shilling minimum wage, a forty-eight hour week, trade union recognition and the abolition of contracting work. It also called for municipal workshops and labour exchanges, the public ownership of gas, electricity, water and tramways and the construction of artisan dwellings, let at rents covering only the cost of building and maintenance. Clearly the NMLU was developing a political perspective beyond their principal concern with employment issues.

A number of leading NMLU activists were by 1894 making their mark in the political arena; Albert James, a flusher and secretary of the No.1 LCC branch won a seat on the Lambeth Vestry and Henry Hodges was elected to the Bermondsey Board of Guardians. As influence on the local election committees grew, so more NMLU candidates were elected and by 1896 there were at least six members representing Labour and Progressive opinion across the metropolis, including John Fitch in Greenwich.

The mid 1890s probably marked the high point in the prominence of the 'labour question', with even the Moderates declaring in their 1896 election manifesto that 'those carrying out public work will not be allowed to practice "sweating" and will pay recognised wages.' This climate was conducive to improvements and the NMLU made real progress. In Battersea, a forty-eight hour week was introduced, Mile End conceded a week's holiday on the instigation of Will Steadman, and a service supplement of one shilling for every year in the Vestry was introduced at Plumstead. A growing number of employers established sick pay schemes, granted permanent status to manual workers and set up procedures for dealing with grievances and dismissals.

Fitch spoke of these advances in 1897:

> All round we may claim to have reduced the hours, raised the wages and secured better conditions of employment generally. Then we

Albin Taylor in 1903.

The financial crisis inside the National Municipal Labour Union intensified in the late 1890s and by March 1899 the general secretary, John Fitch, was advising members of this and cautioning against indiscriminate recruiting.

❛ I regret to say that a great number of (funeral) claims this year are for and from members of just over six months membership … we hope all members know that men desirous of becoming members who are in a serious state of health will not be proposed. ❜

have secured the recognition of the municipal workmen. Four years ago it was dangerous for a vestry employee to agitate for better conditions of work. I was myself dismissed from the Greenwich District Board, of which I am now a member, for agitating. Now, however, things are quite changed. We are recognised as a body to be taken into account.

This assessment was endorsed by the important research carried out by Charles Booth in 1895. Comparing evidence to his earlier study, he found that nearly half of London's municipal employees earned between twenty-five and thirty shillings compared to only one in seven in 1891. Although the study was careful to point out that there were still nearly two hundred municipal employees earning below twenty shillings and that the range of twenty-five to thirty shillings could be included in a measure of poverty, there had been a 'remarkable improvement.' Booth attributed this to the demand that public bodies should be model employers, which had been canvassed so strongly by the NMLU.

The improvement was perhaps most marked among the sweepers. In 1886, the average wage of the London sweeper was nineteen shillings and tuppence but by 1895 it had risen to between twenty-three and twenty-five shillings. Moreover, the status of the sweeper had improved as local authorities were forced to redefine the nature of the work and those performing it. The Kensington surveyor referred to this in 1897 when he said that previously the sweeper's job had been undertaken by 'worn-out and feeble workmen, ousted from their regular employment, and served as a kind of poor relief and acted as a stop-gap on the way to the workhouse.' He went on to contrast this with the modern system where sweepers were expected to be fully able bodied and capable of performing vital public health work.

This sea change was obviously very welcome as it reflected a wider recognition of the importance of municipal labour, but it also meant that many old sweepers were dismissed for not being up to the job. The union protested in these cases, pointing out that the men would inevitably be forced on to relief from the local guardians so becoming a burden on the rate-payers. In one such case in 1897, the union's deputation in support of a sixty-one-year-old Hackney sweeper caused a considerable stir among the elected members. As a magazine scathingly reported, the deputation 'threw the vestry into paroxysms of wrath at such impertinence and interference of a society in Fleet Street' (the NMLU had offices in Fleet Street). The report continued, 'the deputation was ultimately shown the door and the Vestry rubbed their hands and reflected that in their term of office, they had done less work and made more noise than any equal number of men in London.'

Hackney had become a Progressive controlled vestry in 1894, but it still presented serious problems for the NMLU, including the attempted dismissal of one of its activists, Fred Flynn, in 1898. Prompt action by the union forced his reinstatement – albeit with the slimmest of majorities when the issue was heard by the members.

Sharp union action was also necessary in another Progressive Vestry, Newington, in 1895, when the Clerk introduced a piece-rate system for loaders at the central depot. The loaders – who shovelled manure and other sweepings into trucks bound for the Kent countryside – were previously paid four shillings and sixpence a day, which although not a large sum, was more than they could earn under the new piece-rate system. Under the leadership of the Newington Branch of the NMLU, the men took strike action. The Clerk defended his action before the Vestrymen by saying that 'it is a question of whether these men or the Vestry are the masters.'

ASYLUM ATTENDANTS AND THEIR HOURS.

UNDER the auspices of the London County Council Employees Protection Association, a public meeting was held at the Victoria Inn, Boston-road, Hanwell, W., on Friday last. There was a good attendance of the employees at Hanwell Asylum present. Mr. Ben Cooper, L.C.C., was announced to speak, but through indisposition was unable to be present. The General Secretary of the Society, Mr. A. Taylor, delivered a neat and businesslike speech, in which he urged upon the employees the necessity of continued effort. He announced that the Asylums Committee had made one or two small but important concessions, such as facilities for the men to retire after 20 years' service on the 1—60th scale of pension, but the men must be over 50 years of age and not necessarily incapacitated from further service. An extension of the allowance in lieu of rations, when the employees are on sick leave, had been made. The committee were contemplating a reduction in their working hours of about two hours per day. This announcement was received with cheers. Mr. Taylor concluded by making an appeal to the men to be united and solid, and not let personal or sectional jealousies stand in the way.

A hearty vote of thanks being passed to Mr. Taylor and LONDON concluded a thoroughly successful meeting. A resolution was also passed declaring that no method of reducing the hours would be satisfactory which did not allow the men and women two half days per week in addition to the present day per week.

A meeting for the nurses employed at Claybury Asylum will be held on Friday next at the Village Rest, Woodford Bridge, at 8.15 p.m., when Miss Homer Morten and Miss M. Barry will speak, and explain to the nurses the aims and benefits of combination amongst women.

On Tuesday, June 8th, a public meeting will be held at the Bee Hive, New Southgate, N., at 8 15 p.m. sharp, when Messrs. W. C. Steadman, L.C.C., and A. Taylor (General Secretary) will address the meeting. All employees of the L.C.C. at Colney Hatch Asylum are cordially invited to attend.

Albin Taylor and the LCC Employees Protection Association went on a recruiting drive among asylum workers in 1897, often accompanied by a leading Council member close to the union. London, 27 May 1897.

A strike fund was set up to support the loaders and an attempt to bring in strike-breakers from Kent was rebuffed. When the Vestry members met again, it was to discuss a committee report endorsing the actions of the Clerk. The mood of the Vestrymen was overwhelmingly in favour of the strikers, who, as one member remarked, were resisting piece-work which was nothing short of a form of slavery. Another, 'trusted that the members who were returned on the Progressive ticket would stand by the unfortunate depot men and see that they were not sweated any longer.' To roars of laughter, another vestryman remarked that 'Mr Dunham (the Clerk) had not sought in anyway to reduce his own commission by half a ton' and that, 'If any reduction in wages was going to take place, it should start at the top.' Only six votes were recorded in favour of the report and an amendment returning the men to a day rate was carried with rapturous cheering from the union men in the gallery.

The strike was locally organised and directed, although the Executive Council of the NMLU were forced to support it once the men had come out. Fitch didn't like the men taking action without recourse to the union leadership, and the suspicion is that they would have tried to prevent it. Certainly Fitch had removed the episode from his memory two years later when he gave an interview to a magazine and remarked, 'We are in a singularly fortunate position, in so much as we never need to strike and indeed, have never done so, for we have it in our power to get rid of our employers at election time.'

THE LCCEPA

Influencing the employers' attitude was also very much the policy being pursued by Albin Taylor and the fledgling London County Council Employees Protection Association. The 1895 LCC elections had returned an equal number of Progressives and Moderates – although the Progressives retained control because of a greater number of aldermanic seats. A number of Labour members of the LCC were regarded by Taylor as friends of his union, including John Burns, Will Steadman and Will Crooks, and he was optimistic about improvements. Indeed it was important for the LCCEPA to begin to deliver results.

A claim submitted in 1895 on behalf of

Employees of the Metropolitan Water Board breaking ice on the filter beds at the Hampton Works in February 1895.
THAMES WATER

Although the MEA was developing a national character by 1904, its Executive was still dominated by London members. Of the Executive at least four had been active in the National Municipal Labour Union, including Nathaniel Green, an old friend of Taylor's from the West Ham branch since 1892. Green continued as West Ham branch secretary until 1925 when his son Albert took over, to be followed by his son, also Albert, in 1945. The West Ham branch could, therefore, claim until relatively recent times that it had a direct link back to the founders of municipal workers' trade unionism back in the 1890s.

flushers at the Northern Outfall, for reduced hours, pointed out that the fifty-six hour week, spread over seven days, was only exceeded by two authorities in London. The union wanted a forty-eight hour week with no reduction in pay and believed that the conditions under which the men worked justified the improvement. Many of the employees at the Outfall had an hour's walk to and from work and while there they suffered considerable danger and discomfort from the surroundings. One employee described a common experience, 'when a strong, reeking vapour arises from the sludge, which totally envelopes the men and sometimes you cannot see a few feet before you.'

This and other applications for improvements got lost in the complicated LCC com-

mittee structure, and Taylor was forced to raise the issue at the influential London Trades Council, who backed the union's case. The Trades Council also endorsed the LCCEPA claim for a minimum sixty hour week for asylum workers; this group had been joining the union in large numbers following some impressive recruiting by Taylor and his colleagues in 1896. Pressure was applied, and protest meetings were held and in 1897, following an intervention by Will Crooks, the daily hours of attendants were reduced to twelve a day.

But the inability of the LCCEPA to break through on important issues for main drainage staff was, by 1897, beginning to impose strains on the organisation, as membership levelled off at around five hundred, but expenditure continued to increase. One dissatisfied member, an employee at the Northern Outfall, voiced his opinions on Taylor, who had become general secretary in 1896, in the pages of an important municipal journal, 'the Secretary acts upon his own suggestions and sacrifices little of his own time ... he should pay fewer visits to Spring Gardens (the LCC offices) ... the main drainage men started the Association. I am a main drainage man, but have failed to see anything done for the men, despite the General Secretary's promises.' Another LCC employee, this time an asylum worker, jumped to Taylor's defence, emphasising the great deal he risked as General Secretary for the paltry sum of one and a half pence a member per quarter. He suggested that the Northern Outfall member express 'more brotherly feeling and less personal spite'.

But it was true that the LCCEPA had reached an impasse in their relations with the County Council, which threatened to stifle the union. Taylor and the Executive of the LCCEPA had to devise a new approach.

This came in 1899 when the annual meeting decided on the recommendation of the Executive to change the name of the organisation to the National Association of County Authority Employees so giving the scope to activists outside London. It was as a delegate of this organisation that Taylor attended the 1899 TUC where he successfully moved a resolution calling on County Authorities to implement a forty-eight hour week as well as en-

Albin Taylor represented the MEA at the founding conference of the Labour Party in February 1900.

NATIONAL MUSEUM OF LABOUR HISTORY

dorsing parliamentary action to improve the conditions of asylum workers.

THE MUNICIPAL EMPLOYEES ASSOCIATION

In November 1899 the Executive were once again inviting delegates to revise the title, this time to the Municipal Employees Association (MEA). Membership was growing again and now stood at 600 and but it was soon to be boosted by a sequence of events reverberating through the National Municipal Labour Union.

The financial insecurity of the NMLU had been recognised as early as 1893, when it became clear that heavy demands were being made through funeral benefit claims. As membership declined in the following years, the problem became more acute but no reforms were made. By the end of 1898, the situation was reaching crisis proportions and the General Secretary, John Fitch, was appealing to the members to do something – either in the form of an age limit for new recruits, increased contributions, or a reduced funeral benefit. Once again no action was taken and the union appeared to be struck by a paralysis – either unable or unwilling to make the necessary changes. Debts piled up and in August 1899 a special enquiry discovered a deficiency of more than £300 in the accounts, which was attributed to Fitch. The Executive Council dismissed him from office and took out a summons in the courts to re-

cover the money. At the trial in September, Fitch admitted he had been careless with money, but claimed responsibility should be shared between all the NMLU officials. The Court held him responsible and ordered him to pay back the £300 or go to prison for two months. We do not know if the money was ever paid back, but it seems very unlikely.

Fitch was succeeded as General Secretary by his assistant Herbert Day, a nineteen-year-old who had joined the union as an office boy in 1893. Facing an almost impossible task, this young man and the Executive Council convened a special delegate meeting which agreed to a special levy and an age limit of fifty-five years for new members qualifying for funeral benefit. Regrettably these changes had little impact, as members were losing faith in the organisation, and refusing to act on the instructions. Branches in Camberwell, Hackney and Westminster broke away and formed local societies, while others began to collapse.

The final body blow occurred in August 1900 when Herbert Day was found to have embezzled £100 from the union and, like Fitch, was taken to court and fined. A new General Secretary was appointed, a Hackney member, George Hibbard, but he had no chance of rescuing the union at this stage and by the end of 1900 it was no longer operating. Even the Registrar of Friendly Societies had great difficulty in finding a responsible officer of the union to confirm the

Will Steadman, a loyal supporter of municipal workers' trade unionism from 1889 until his death in 1911. He was a member of the Mile End Vestry, London County Council, and twice a Member of Parliament. He advised the Vestry Employees Union, The London County Council Protection Association and acted as President of the MEA from 1903 to 1906.

Successful negotiations, like this described by Taylor in 1904, encouraged tramway workers employed by the LCC to join the MEA. By 1906 there were fifteen branches catering for tramway workers across London.

demise in order that the name could be removed from the register of trade unions.

Albin Taylor and the leadership of the MEA watched events in the NMLU very closely, aware of future membership potential – which was soon realised, as some five hundred NMLU members came over.

These were quickly followed by the well administered Battersea Society, which had been independent since 1894, and whose members could boast the best wages and conditions in the capital. The MEA now had a reasonably free hand in London – apart from pockets of Gas Workers' influence such as Poplar – and it set about recruiting and absorbing the remaining independent societies.

The Municipal Employees Association established a 30 shillings a week minimum wage for employees in London (and 28 shillings in provincial areas) based on the average cost of living in 1903:

	£	s	d
Rent	0	7	6
Coal and light	0	2	6
Clothes and boots for man and family	0	3	0
Additions and renewals to furniture	0	2	0
Sick Clubs etc	0	1	0
Food and other necessities for the whole family	0	14	0
Theatres and other enlightenment	Nil		
	£1 10s 0d		

❝Can anyone suggest a more economical way than this of living on 30 shillings per week in London? We strongly suggest that a man who is wiling to do the filthy and arduous work of cleansing and repairing the roads, cleaning urinals, doing the garden and constabulary work etc, etc, is worthy of a decent home and good food and clothes, and ought to now and then be able to go to the theatre and otherwise enjoy themselves.❞ Albin Taylor, 1903

But Taylor was aware that the future of the MEA could only be secured with recruitment outside of London, and this became the prime task. Organising tours were undertaken by the General Secretary, and Battersea branch secretary Albert Winfield, both men taking leave from work to visit the West Country, East Midlands and the North West. New branches were set up and the MEA began to get a foothold in the important cities of Bristol, Leicester, Nottingham and Manchester. Taylor began to see the potential of a truly national union of municipal employees as membership reached 3000 in 1902.

The increased work-load made it necessary for the MEA to appoint a full time General Secretary and Taylor was duly elected at the special delegate meeting in 1902, but only after a long and complicated debate about the terms of his contract. Members feared a repeat of the events which had torn the NMLU apart, while Taylor was conscious of the possibility of cliques forming on the Executive and dismissing him. A £100 guarantee was set aside and would be paid to Taylor if the union failed to meet its liabilities or if he were defeated in an election.

The union's long standing problems with the LCC continued and the claim that the Council was a model employer infuriated the MEA. It had ample evidence to present showing the true LCC record on labour questions. The thirty shilling minimum which was accepted by a growing number of local authorities across London was rejected time after time by the LCC, despite the efforts of the union's loyal friend Will Steadman. The union published the shocking fact that LCC 'charwomen' were in 1904 paid as little as fifteen shillings a week, compared to Battersea's thirty shillings. The original architect of the Council's labour policy, and opponent of the thirty shilling minimum, Sidney Webb, held the Deptford seat, where the union had several hundred members – provoking Taylor to write in his report on 1902 that 'the municipal employees of Deptford are asleep and doing nothing to return a true friend of labour.'

Seemingly above the ranks of the manual labourers in the Council's workforce were the firemen and park constables – but uniform and status didn't prevent these workers from recognising their need for a union and joining the MEA after 1900.

Despite hostility from the Council, who threatened to dismiss firemen for taking grievances through union channels, the branch grew rapidly and by 1906 had more than four hundred in membership. Their battle for recognition was to simmer for a few years before exploding in 1918.

A more immediate struggle faced the park constables, who in July 1903 were ordered by the Council to collect litter as part of their duties. These were proud men – typically ex-army NCOs and ex-policemen – and this they regarded as menial work below their important office as law enforcers in the Council's parks. They simply refused to collect litter, resulting in the Council suspending fifty-one of them. The MEA took up the case and advised the men to perform the extra duties under protest, while a union deputation put the case before the Parks Committee. The Committee did not receive the union representatives until three months after the dispute had started and by this time any momentum had been lost and so, with it, the park constables' case. In encouraging the men to work normally the MEA was demonstrating that it suffered from the same weakness as the NMLU when it came to using industrial action as part of the union's armoury. Like its predecessor, the MEA would proudly state in an appeal for members in 1905: 'We do not advocate strikes or lock outs, but give our members their money back, which would be used in this way in death benefits.'

The MEA's cautious industrial approach contrasted with its aggressive recruiting tactics – a mixture sure to incur the wrath of

BELFAST.—We organized two Mass Meetings of all grades of employees in this City, on January 4th and 5th. At the close of the speeches the following Resolutions were enthusiastically carried.

(1) That this Mass Meeting of the Citizens of Belfast hereby respectfully appeals to the Belfast Corporation to pay to its Employees a minimum wage of 28s. per week, seeing that this is the lowest sum on which a man can bring up a family in decency in Belfast.

(2) That no Employee work more than 48 hours per week.

(3) And further, appeals to all the Corporation Employees to Organize and become Trades Unionists, so that they would become a powerful factor in obtaining the above conditions of employment.

We followed this up with questions to candidates at the Municipal Elections and those who pledge themselves to support these principles (if returned) to the City Council, and every Corporation employee urged to do all he could to secure their return.

competing unions. The Gas Workers Union, in particular, objected to the MEA treading on its toes and accused Taylor of leading a 'pudding club', which could pay out high benefits to members because it never fought disputes. Taylor delighted in replying to these accusations, aware that they reflected an expansion into the heartlands of the two general unions, who also recruited municipal employees – the Gas Workers Union and the National Amalgamated Labour Union.

THE UNION EXPANDS

Recruitment went on apace as Taylor and others undertook organising expeditions, but it became clear in 1904 that new members meant more work for the sole full-time official, who the Executive believed was dangerously over-working himself. He needed an assistant and in July Richard Davies, a Leicester man with a trade union background, was appointed on Taylor's recommendation.

Davies quickly showed his recruiting abilities in Glasgow, where in a few months he was successful in establishing nine branches with 1500 members. Members of the Glasgow Pipe Layers and Jointers Association came over to the MEA *en bloc* with their secretary

As membership grew, independent local unions were drawn into the MEA. One of these, the Belfast Municipal Employees and Other Workers Society, joined in November 1905 and reports of its meetings were included in the Journal.

As the Municipal Employees Association grew and began to take in a wide range of local authority employees, such as tramway workers, it came up against opposition from other unions, as Albin Taylor related to members in 1905:

❝ The Secretary of our Manchester No 2 Branch, the Motormen and Conductors Branch, reports as follows: I was approached by Mr W Totitt on Friday who asked me if I was prepared to come over to the Tramway and Vehicle Workers Union, he is the President of that body, and he had no doubt he could make it worth my while. However, it didn't come off. Query: What do you municipal tramway men think of tactics of this sort, and what do the officials of other trade unions think of it, or the Parliamentary committee of the Trades Union Congress? I am afraid a straightforward trade unionist would call it contemptible. ❞

Leaflet issued by Taylor following the 1906 TUC which condemned separate unions for public service workers.

Trade Union Congress, Liverpool, 1906.

MUNICIPAL QUESTIONS.

GENTLEMEN,

The unskilled Municipal Workers of the country claim the right to have a Union of their own, financed and officered by themselves, and carrying out a policy which they may determine from time to time for the following and other reasons :—

1. To get information about one another.

2. To bring about more Uniform Conditions of Service in the various towns for each class of work.

3. By being all together we are stronger than by being divided into many Societies.

4. We could then use our Collective Influence to secure the return of a still larger number of Labour Candidates.

5. We claim to know the way to deal with Municipal Employment better than those who have never worked for a public body.

6. We have never been catered for properly by other Societies, and they have failed to keep the men in their Unions.

7. What difference can it make to the Labour Movement whether Municipal Workers have a Union of their own or be in with the G.W. & G.L.U., the A.A. of T. & V.W., or the A.U. of L., so long as they are represented at this Congress, the Labour Party, and on Trades Councils as we are, also Registered as a Trade Union ? The only difference is we as a Municipal Workers' Association gets the men's money instead of the above Unions

8 We are very desirous of working with and forming a part of the Great Labour Movement, meet our dues and do our share of the work, but we certainly claim the right to a Society of our own.

9. Much controversy is going on among Officials of Trade Unions that we allow Mechanics to join us. We would ask those who have direct evidence of this to submit such evidence to us, when we will do the right thing, as we hold the view most strongly that Mechanics ought to belong to their own Trade Union. No one has proved to us a case yet : we have had several innuendoes but no facts.

10. The officials of these Unions and their emissaries have obstructed us in every town we go to to organize the Municipal Workers. We will take one sample, viz., Bristol. We found about 200, out of 1,300 employed in the Gas Workers' Union ; they said we object to you coming into this town to even organize the 1,100 remaining outside as they are our preserves. (We suppose they had them in pickle). This same line has been pursued all along for years, although we state we do not ask any man to leave any other Union to join ours, and we frequently put it on our handbills We have brought into the movement about 16,000 men and women, the chief of whom were outside it. Had we got these into the G.W. & G.L.U., the A.A. of T. & V.W , or the A.U. of L., instead of into a Society of our own, we should have been acclaimed

11. Very few private firms employ men to do the same work as Public Bodies do, take Sweepers, Dustmen, Sewermen, Pickers, Steam Roller Drivers, Fire Brigades, Parks Employees, Cemetery Employees, Lunatic Asylum Employees, &c., &c., as examples.

12. We always understood the purpose of the T.U.C. was to bring all Trade Unions together, and not to define what trades or occupations should or should not have a Union of their own.

Faithfully yours,

A. TAYLOR, *General Secretary,*

Municipal Employees' Association,

923, Romford Road, London, E.

John Martin becoming the first full-time regional organiser of the MEA.

With membership growing so rapidly, the MEA was able to update and introduce benefits to members, including a death benefit rising to ten pounds after fourteen years membership. A significant financial surplus was returned by the union in 1904 and the President Will Steadman told members:

You are the strongest organisation that has ever existed on behalf of municipal employees. I can justify that statement by saying that I have taken a great interest in the organisation of municipal employees ever since the first branch was started in Camberwell fourteen years ago.

Evoking the memory of the Camberwell pio-

*Westminster City Council
employees, c 1900.*
WESTMINSTER CITY COUNCIL LIBRARIES

neers in 1904 was opportune, because the MEA was keen to bring back into a wider organisation those local societies who had broken away from the NMLU as it was declining. By 1906 the Camberwell members had voted to go in with the MEA, following the Hackney, Wimbledon, Westminster and Southwark societies some years earlier. With these transfers, trade unionism amongst municipal workers in London was once again under a unified banner.

The growing prominence of the MEA helped Taylor and Davies attract other local societies, including the Hull Corporation Employees Protection Society and the Belfast Municipal Employees and Other Workers Trade Union in 1905. The MEA was now developing into a national organisation and this needed to be reflected in the structure of the union. In particular, places needed to be allocated on the Executive Council to members outside London. The country was, accordingly, divided up into districts, each with its own semi-autonomous conference, which

elected the Executive member. The London dominance on the Executive was thus ended.

Further expansion in Manchester and Stockport enabled an additional district secretary, Peter Tevenan, to be appointed and this was soon followed by a London post for Albert Winfield. Richard Davies took on the district secretary's job for the South Western and Wales district, while in Belfast Andrew Boyd, the former secretary of the local society, became the union's full-time officer.

With these changes the MEA was by the beginning of 1906 geared up for a major expansion. Membership already stood at 16,000 and the general unions knew that they faced a formidable competitor in the MEA, so much so that at the 1906 TUC in Liverpool, the National Amalgamated Labour Union and the Gas Workers Union proposed a motion condemning trade unionism which divided public service workers from those in the private sector. Accusations were made against the union, and Albin Taylor in particular, for 'intimidating' labour councillors to induce

MUNICIPAL WORKERS' SOCIETY.

(Established to promote and protect the interests of Municipal Servants.)

Offices—7, THORPE ROAD, EAST HAM, LONDON, E.

Although unable to prove their dreadful (*sic!*) charges at the London Conference on March 9th, Mr. Taylor's suspension by the vote of the Chairman was confirmed by 11 to 10 (3 remaining neutral), at Manchester, on the 16th. In view of this unjust and unwarranted conduct, Branches with from 4,000 to 5,000 Members have seceded to form the above Society with your old leader, **tried and true,** as Secretary.

YOU SHOULD DO THE SAME FORTHWITH BECAUSE:—

1.—Every lover of fair play and justice must condemn the above action.

2. -All Benefits will be guaranteed to every Member who transfers as though nothing had happened. **We will not see the Members suffer a financial loss.**

3.—You should support the man who has successfully for 14 years fought your battles and gained some splendid concessions before the present managers of affairs were known to you.

4. You should not support a Society whose Chief Officials never worked as Municipal Servants and therefore cannot properly understand the work.

5.—About £20,000 has passed through Mr. Taylor's hands during his official career in the Labour Movement, **and the Chartered Accountants certify that not a Penny has gone wrong.**

6.—By having a smaller Society your Secretary could be with you more.

7.—Mr. Taylor was ousted from his office after 14 years, he being the founder, without any written and signed charge being submitted against him, although he asked for this so that he could meet and answer his accusers.

8.—The London District, where Mr. Taylor's work is best known, which has over 7,000 members, was only entitled to **four** Delegates, whilst the Manchester, North Eastern, Scottish and Irish Districts, with only about 7,000 members in all, had **sixteen** delegates. The delegates from the London, Manchester and West of England Districts who voted were for Mr. Taylor ; there are about 11,000 members in these Districts, or about two-thirds the total membership.

9.—Pay all future Contributions into the above Society. **All Benefits Guaranteed.**

Look at the Benefits you get in this Society for the following small Contributions, viz.

MEN.—Entrance Fee 1/-, Rule Book 3d., Contribution Card 1d. each year, and 2½d. per week as Contributions.

WOMEN AND YOUTHS.—Entrance Fee 6d., Rule Book 3d., Contribution Card 1d. each year, and 1½d. per week as Contributions, and be entitled to Half the Funeral Claims and Half the Accident Benefit as shown in the Rules, or they may pay Full Entrance Fee of 1/- and 2½d. per week and be entitled to Full Benefits.

Any eligible Municipal Servant may join the Society by remitting his or her Contributions to the Head Office, 7, Thorpe Road, East Ham, London, E, Monthly or Quarterly.

☞ BENEFITS. ☜

1.—Legal Protection.

2.—£100 should you meet with an Accident whilst at work which permanently disables you from following any employment.

3.—In case you meet with an Accident, and the person causing it is unable to pay your loss, we can assist you from the funds up to £10.

4.—Up to £10 in case of your death.

5.—Up to £5 in case of your wife's death.

6.—Efforts are made to bring about equal Wages, Hours, Holidays, &c., for each grade of work.

7.—Facts as to Wages, Hours, Holidays, &c., of your fellow workmen in other districts.

8.—A Superannuation Bill is promoted to ensure pensions to all Municipal Servants.

9.—Petitions are presented and applications made for better wages, shorter hours, holidays, &c.

10.—In case you are punished or dismissed and you think it unjust, we enquire into it, advise and assist you.

11.—A Report is issued *Free* quarterly to inform you what the Society is doing, &c.

In what other Society can you get such benefits for 2½d. per week ?

SICK SECTION (Voluntary).

Any Branch with twenty members, who have passed a Medical examination, may allow them to join this Section. *Contributions* 4d. *per week.* After six months' membership each member is entitled to 10/- per week for 8 weeks, and 5/- per week for a further 4 weeks, on being unable to follow employment through Sickness or Accident.

MUTUAL GUARANTEE FUND (Voluntary).

Any Branch may establish this Fund, each Member who joins pays 6d. at the death of any other member of the fund. All the money is paid to the Members dependents.

Note.—1,000 sixpences make £25 ; 2,000 £50, 3,000 £75 ; 4,000 £100 ; 5,000 £125.

A. TAYLOR, General Secretary.

council employees to leave other unions and join the MEA. Unfortunately Taylor was unwell and could not reply, leaving the job to Albert Winfield and Peter Tevenan. Both emphasised the right of municipal employees to have their own union like other groups of workers. The arguments, however, cut no ice with the delegates, who were lined up against the MEA and supported the motion. The TUC was therefore obliged to advise trades councils, unions and the Labour Party, that municipal employees' unions 'have a weak-

ening and disintegrating effect upon the forces of organised labour.'

With these instructions circulating, the immediate future was going to be very difficult for the MEA. Events unfolding inside the union were to compound these problems and create a historic rift in municipal workers' trade unionism.

INTERNAL DISPUTES

The origin of the dispute can be traced back to a series of complaints from branches in

The MEA Journal for June 1906 reported with great delight on the growth of the union in Glasgow:

❛ Such is fate – The Conservative Club in George Street, Glasgow became closed through lack of support. The MEA has stepped in and taken over the premises, and in place of the photo of Mr Balfour [Conservative leader] & Co, will hang the photos of our Officers. ❜

the North West about the activities and behaviour of district secretary Peter Tevenan. These were investigated by the Executive and were regarded as serious enough for him to be dismissed in December 1906. Tevenan moved to establish a breakaway organisation based in the North East which Taylor quickly countered by sending the district secretaries to the area to present the MEA's case. Richard Davies – at this time working in Scotland – met Tevenan, against Taylor's instructions, and went to see the Executive Council Chairman Richard Baldwin in Leicester. Davies was able to convince Baldwin that it was the General Secretary and not Tevenan who was at fault and at the next meeting of the Executive in January 1907, Tevenan was reinstated and, remarkably, fifty pounds was given towards the expenses of floating the breakaway union. Motions flooded into the office from branches, some calling for Taylor's resignation and others urging the Executive to stick by the General Secretary.

A special Executive meeting was held in February 1907 at which Taylor faced allegations of acting in defiance of the Executive and issuing circulars which vilified members of that body. His spirited defence proved of no avail as the Executive approved by a two to one majority a resolution to suspend Taylor. The meeting then appointed Richard Davies as temporary General Secretary and called a special delegate conference for March to endorse their actions. The tables had been turned with Taylor now the accused.

The delegate meeting in March allowed Taylor to defend himself before the activists, although he subsequently claimed he only saw the charges on the day of the conference itself and could not, therefore, prepare properly. Evidence was produced which showed Taylor had become frustrated with the actions of the Executive and had urged district secretaries to find replacement members. He claimed this circular had subsequently been withdrawn, but by then the damage had been

done. Davies and other district secretaries wanted Taylor out and the circular was damming evidence.

It was also alleged that Taylor had caused great injury to the MEA by submitting an amendment to the general unions' motion at the 1906 TUC. The amendment stated that far from municipal workers' trade unions being against the interests of trade unionism, it was in fact against the financial interests of the unions proposing the motion – including the National Amalgamated Labour Union and the Gas Workers Union. Presenting the case for the Executive, Davies claimed that Taylor refused to withdraw the amendment, ignoring the advice of the other MEA delegates (three full-time district secretaries), and then on the day it was to be discussed left congress claiming to be ill. Certainly the amendment was provocative and characteristic of Taylor's approach, but it must be remembered that the general unions were gunning for the MEA and were capable of mustering enough votes in their favour irrespective of the MEA's response.

After thirteen hours of charge and counter-charge the twenty four delegates moved to a vote and decided by eleven votes to ten – with three abstentions – to back the Executive.

Within ten days Taylor and his longstanding friends from London had convened a conference to establish a new organisation – the Municipal Workers Society. London branches started to leave the MEA and join the new union as did five West Country branches. The MEA put as many obstacles in the way of Taylor as possible, including objecting to the title of the new organisation, claiming it was too close to that of the Municipal Employees Association. The National Union of Corporation Workers was found to be an acceptable alternative and so within weeks of being dismissed as general secretary of one municipal workers' trade union, Taylor was in charge of another.

3. The Corporation Workers

1907-25

Tom McGrath of St. Marylebone. He had been active in the MEA, won a seat on the Corporation Workers Executive, became President in 1912, and in 1918 was appointed Assistant General Secretary. He died in 1921.

THE NUCW

During the MEA dispute, Albin Taylor revealed personal characteristics which contributed to his downfall. He was certainly capable of grave errors of judgement as he displayed in circulating a letter to district secretaries criticising Executive Council members. He also found it difficult to recognise that as the union grew, it would need to develop a structure and organisation beyond the personality of an individual leader. This often meant that his leadership was autocratic and he alienated potential allies.

But he was also a leader who commanded loyalty and support and this was at its strongest amongst the London members who knew him well and followed him into the National Union of Corporation Workers (NUCW) in 1907.

The task of building a new national union on the foundations of 3500 London members plus a few hundred in the provinces could not have been undertaken at a more difficult time. The union was naturally excluded from the TUC and the Labour Party, for the same reasons that the MEA was soon to be jettisoned, implementing the 1906 TUC decision that municipal workers' trade unionism was divisive. The MEA itself attacked the Corporation Workers at every opportunity, singling out Taylor as the villain of the piece. Taylor for his part made sure that

it was a two-way dialogue issuing denunciations and 'exposures' of the MEA. When the arbitrators deciding on whether he should be paid the £100 guarantee cleared him on a number of MEA charges, and awarded in his favour, he extracted maximum publicity value from the decision.

The Corporation Workers also faced a hostile response from the employers at municipal level, particularly in London. Against the national trend, which had seen a Liberal government elected with a large majority (and a significant number of Labour members) in 1906, London politics turned to the right, with a municipal reform (Tory) majority at the LCC and in many London borough councils. (Borough councils superseded vestries in 1900.)

Claiming a primary responsibility to the rate-payer, councils set on a drive for 'economy', which the union correctly perceived as a euphemism for an attack on pay and conditions. In Edmonton, the home town of Henry Bye, NUCW organiser since 1908, the thirty shilling minimum wage was abolished. Lewisham and East Ham attempted to introduce contractors for dust and sweeping, only to be out-manoeuvred by NUCW-inspired campaigns which brought together a wide spectrum of opposition. Bye and Taylor were able to characterise contracting as an outdated Victorian practice which had no place in

The union tradition of intervening in local politics was carried forward into the Corporation Workers Union when it was set up in 1907. The London organiser, Henry Bye, a socialist candidate in the 1908 borough council elections in Edmonton, made the connection between politics and trade unionism when he reported to members:

❛ During the campaign I had a shock. I approached a road sweeper and solicited his vote, his reply was: 'No, I have never voted yet and never will, what good can Labour men do me?' This man is in receipt of 30 shillings per week, twelve years ago he received 18 shillings for the same work, and today the present reactionary Council have threatened to reduce these old men from 30 shillings to 25 shillings per week. Comment is superfluous. ❜

the modern local authority. Chelsea Borough Council were less responsive to union pressure and went ahead with a series of changes which reduced the status of workers from weekly to hourly paid employees and gave the foreman the right to hire and fire.

The LCC, now under Municipal Reform control, merely carried on with the poor labour policy – in respect of unskilled manual labour – set by the Progressives since 1889.

The thirty shilling minimum was again rejected, holidays with pay were only granted to men in fire brigade workshops and tramway workers, and recognition was refused to the NUCW in the fire brigade. The Council's once proud Works Department was run down and closed in 1909.

If a number of influential authorities were keen to reverse advances achieved since 1889, others simply carried on as if trade unions had never existed. That hardy perennial Paddington, continued to ignore deputations from the union on the grounds that they consisted of outsiders agitating among the men. Holborn also continued to be a thorn in the side of the NUCW, the Council persisting in its paternalistic relationship with the employees, and providing an annual sup-

per at which there was singing of 'Land of Hope and Glory', a toast to 'The King' and speeches from employees, thanking the councillors for their generosity.

If the Corporation Workers had problems in the capital, nothing prevented them from looking for new ground. Taylor and his organiser Henry Bye went back on the road and set up meetings for asylum workers in the Home Counties, such as at Napsbury in Hertfordshire, where they found attendants still working an eighty-four hour week. Things were not much better in the LCC asylums, but the NUCW organisers were able to point to a reduced working week and a more relaxed regime for those living in as improvements won by the union. If it were possible, many employees of the Boards of Guardians – responsible for poor relief – had still worse conditions. Nurses of the Edmonton Board worked one hundred hours a week with a daily regime stretching from 5.45 am until 10.00 pm. Poor law branches were set up, claims for improvements made, and slowly wages and conditions crept into the twentieth century – albeit twenty years after everyone else.

Taylor was also always on the look out for

Workers involved in 'public health' in the London area continued to be the dominant force in the Corporation Workers Union.

LONDON BOROUGH OF CAMDEN

"ASKING FOR MORE."

Exeter Street Sweeper: "Please, Sir, can I have a rise of a shilling? I'm only getting 18 bob a week!"
Shocked Councillor: "How can we afford it? We have only recently decided to give the Town Clerk 86s. a week extra, and must economise in the lower grades to make up for it!"
At the last meeting of the City Council a petition was received from the street sweepers asking for a general increase of 1s. a week.

The Exeter branch was one of the outposts of organisation for the Corporation Workers Union in 1914.

discontented MEA branches and when approached by the Edinburgh members in 1909, brought them quickly within the fold of the Corporation Workers, giving the new union its first members in Scotland. The Edinburgh branch was unique in trade union terms in that it was developing an embryonic industrial complexion, as employees from all departments – cleansing, tramways, electricity, gas – and all grades joined the NUCW.

Although excluded from the Labour Party, the Corporation Workers continued to plough money into the electoral field. With manifestos stressing the need for all authorities to recognise a thirty shilling minimum wage in London and a twenty-five shilling elsewhere, a forty-eight hour week and better sickness and holiday arrangements, the union was able to project itself as an important factor in municipal politics. Even where

the Labour and Progressive interest was not great, the union would flood the constituency with publicity, hoping to put the 'labour question' back at the top of the agenda, a position it had not enjoyed for over a decade. In St. Pancras, 50,000 leaflets were issued in the 1912 borough council elections listing those Moderates who voted against a pay increase for poorly paid employees.

Taylor appealed to the voters:

Workers, remember their names when you go to the poll on Friday November 1st.

Citizens of St. Pancras! This niggardly policy is carried out in your name! Do you desire to continue? The day has gone for less than trade union rates.

Moderates are sweaters; out em.

The union's extensive political work was paid

Following the decision of the 1906 TUC to condemn municipal workers' trade unions as divisive, the Corporation Workers were excluded from the TUC and the Labour Party. Jim Bradley, the NUCW president in 1911, commented on this:

❛ What is this terrible thing we demand? Simply the same right that the engineers, the railway servants and all other trades have. The right to combine among themselves and have a union of their own… The alleged reason they give is, that for Municipal Workers to organise into a union of their own 'is detrimental to the interests of trade unionism'… It will not do. The real reason, methinks, lies much nearer the pockets of some person or persons who shout 'Workers of the world unite', but unless you leave your fellows whose interests are bound up with your own, you are not united. You cannot be properly united in a union founded, managed and officered by men who understand and can feel your hardships and wants. To be united you must split yourselves up into different societies where no one understands your peculiar conditions and knows nothing of your aspirations – and don't care. Could absurdity go further? ❜

for out of a fund raised by a separate levy on members. This allowed the NUCW to maintain its policy of influencing local authorities through the ballot box while other unions suffered under the Osborne judgement, which outlawed trade unions' using money from their general funds for political purposes.

If the Osborne judgement was forcing unions to reconsider their political activity, a new trend within the labour movement was also raising questions about the value of electoral work. Syndicalism grew in the period of industrial unrest in the years between 1910 and 1914, and appealed to workers not to look to established party politics to change society, but to the militant trade unions, amalgamated on industrial lines. This movement had its adherents within the Corporation Workers, including the Executive Council member from Bethnal Green, Jim Bradley. At the 1912 annual conference, Bradley, as President of the Union, referred to the new solidarity of workers that had emerged and which provided great possibilities:

> a new era is opening up before us in which the old divisions of skilled and unskilled are done with, and in which all classes of labour, including clerks and civil servants are organising for new economic conditions.

Bradley received support from those delegates who were also influenced by syndicalism, and were bringing repeated calls for amalgamation of municipal workers' unions to the floor of the annual conference. Taylor,

although in principle in favour of one union for municipal workers – as long as it was his union – did not believe the conditions were right for amalgamation, and at the 1913 conference, in a major debate, was able to convince delegates that the militant stance demanded by the syndicalists offered no way forward.

STRIKE ACTIVITY
Taylor stuck by his view that

> There are two ways of conducting a trade union. One is by employing officers to secure concessions by argument and reason (we do this) the second is by leaving the members to pay and fight their own battles through strikes.

Corporation Workers members were prepared to support Taylor for the time being, but it was a policy which did not survive the war, which broke out in the summer of 1914.

Membership in 1914 had grown to 8500 as recruiting efforts began to pay dividends, with new branches established in West Yorkshire, Lancashire and Nottinghamshire. Edinburgh could claim 900 members and was second only in size to the London Fire Brigade branch who had topped the thousand mark.

As new branches were set up during the war years, claims for a war bonus were submitted to compensate for the steeply rising cost of living. Between 1914 and 1919 prices more than doubled and, although bonuses were won in a large number of authorities,

Walter Conquer of Tottenham. Active in the MEA, he was a close friend of Albin Taylor and so went with him into the Corporation Workers Union in 1907. He served as President from 1915-17 and subsequently was a Trustee for many years, until his death in 1941. He presented two shields to the union, to be awarded to branches with the best recruiting record, and he aslo donated the Presidential chain of office.

As the range of municipal services grew, opportunities for recruiting new groups of workers emerged. Among these were public baths attendants such as shown here in the Leyton baths in 1910.

VESTRY HOUSE MUSEUM, WALTHAMSTOW

they often lagged behind increases in the cost of living. Frustration inevitably built up and by 1918, as the war moved towards a conclusion, workers in the municipal services seemed prepared to take action in defence of their living standards.

Taylor and the Executive Council were now more responsive to these developments; in the summer of 1918 the NUCW issued strike threats to several London boroughs who refused to concede a one pound war bonus. All but one gave in to the ultimatum and the union claimed a series of victories. Holborn, however, remained steadfast, forcing the union to call members out on strike. The strike was solid from the first day, with effective picketing resisting the introduction of street sweeping contractors. Faced with such determination, the authority conceded the

demand and the strike was won. Successful strikes were also led by the Corporation Workers in Pontefract in 1919 and Rochdale in 1920, providing evidence that industrial action was an invaluable tool to apply sharp pressure on intransigent employers.

If the Corporation Workers were beginning to do some thinking about their strike policy, so were parts of the employers' establishment, who began to recognise the dangers that may arise when public services were not being provided. Suggesting that the Ministry of Health ought to take action, the Medical Correspondent of *The Times* newspaper commented in 1919 that strikes by street sweepers 'should have never been allowed to occur. These men are part of the police force whose duty it is to keep order against disease … the strike is equivalent to a refusal by a

The Corporation Workers had a number of long running disputes with the general unions, most notably over the exclusion of the NUCW from representation on the East and West Midlands JICs. In the context of this dispute, Albin Taylor spoke in support of a motion at the 1924 TUC, calling on the General Council to prevent disputes between unions by referring them to a Disputes Committee. He said:

❝ I hope that if this resolution is passed the General Council will make a serious effort to secure fair play and justice given on the facts, regardless of what persons or organisations may be concerned. I am very suspicious in this matter, and I sincerely hope that it will not be possible for large bodies of persons to have their way because of their numbers. If allegations are made against a union they should be proved, and if persons are guilty they should be punished – but only if they are guilty – and the people whose duty it is to judge should have a fair and impartial mind and consider the matter fairly and squarely. ❞

nurse or doctor to attend a case of severe sickness.' The implication was that strikes should be made illegal in the public health services, and as we shall see, this idea was taken up by the government some years later.

Another group of NUCW members involved in life and death work – certainly of a more direct kind – were the London firemen. Since 1905 they had petitioned the LCC for recognition but on each occasion had been turned away on the grounds that trade unionism interfered with the relationship between the firemen and their superior officers. In 1913 the Chief Officer had advised the Council to dismiss the union's branch secretary, E.W. Southgate, a working fireman, which prompted the NUCW to allow Jim Bradley, an LCC park-keeper, to become the men's spokesman. Bradley had a special affinity with the service, in that his father had been a London fireman and he himself had been born in a fire station. So when the union again took up the question of recognition in the autumn of 1918, Bradley took the leading role, this time presenting the Council with a more militant stance involving a possible strike. The Council refused to give way and the Government's Chief Industrial Commissioner Sir George Askwith was brought in.

During meetings with Bradley and the LCC representatives, Askwith detected that the Council might be prepared to recognise an independent Fireman's Trade Union divorced entirely from the NUCW. Bradley saw merit in this idea and so it became the basis of the Commissioner's award in September.

Taylor had not been involved in the detailed discussions – indeed Bradley deliberately kept him in the dark – so when the award was made, he was naturally furious. By this time, however, it was too late – Bradley had set out plans for a new body, so depriving the Corporation Workers of over one thousand members, and striking a severe blow against the union's aspiration to represent all grades of local authority employees.

Despite this setback, membership continued to grow, and by 1920 it stood at a record 16,500 – many of the most recent recruits emerging from the clerical grades as they too began to join trade unions to improve their wages and conditions. This breadth of membership helped give the union the status it needed as it entered into talks with employers' organisations about the structure and representation of the joint industrial councils (JICs) being established in the years 1918-22.

JOINT INDUSTRIAL COUNCILS

The idea for JICs had emerged out of a government committee, headed by the House of Commons Speaker J.H. Whitley. The Committee recommended a system of councils of employers and union representatives, who could reach joint decisions on pay and conditions and resolve grievances between them. The idea was taken up enthusiastically by the official representatives of the local authorities

East Ham County Borough Council Election, 1919.

CENTRAL WEST WARD.

POLLING DAY:

Saturday, November 1st, 8 a.m. to 8 p.m.

Vote for the REAL LABOUR CANDIDATE,

A. TAYLOR,

with Thirty Years Official Experience,

Committee Rooms : 103 WAKEFIELD STREET.

Printed and Published by A. SUCKLING (T.U.), 156 High Street, East Ham.

Deselected by the local Labour Party because of his support for a Liberal in the 1918 general election – there was no Labour candidate – Taylor stood as the 'real Labour candidate' in the 1919 borough council elections. Despite nine years' service as a councillor and member of the Metropolitan Water Board he was defeated by the official Labour candidate.

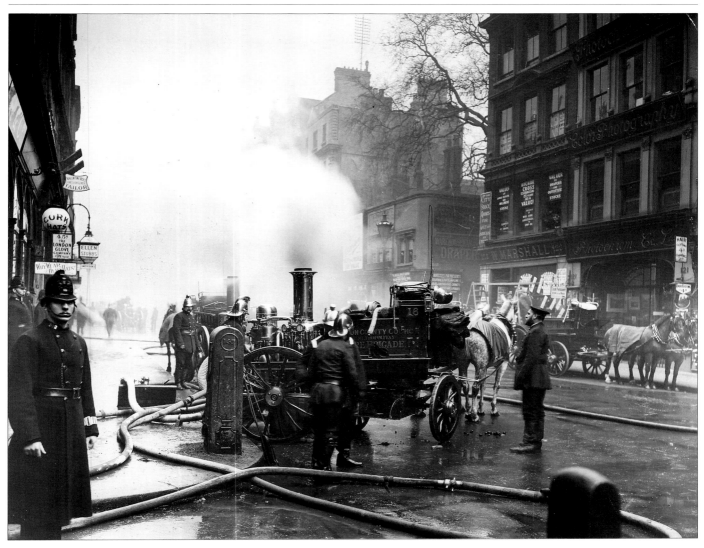

London firemen employed by the LCC began joining the MEA in 1905, transferring to the Corporation Workers two years later. By 1913 the branch had 1100 members but could still not win recognition. This only came in 1918, following a strike threat, when the firemen broke away to form a representative body which eventually helped form the Fire Brigades Union. The Corporation Workers and NUPE continued to have some fire brigade members in Edinburgh and Aberdeen. The photo shows London firemen in action at the turn of the century.

and the trade unions, and by 1919 a National Joint Industrial Council was established for manual workers – referred to as the non-trading services. Soon after, regional or provincial bodies were established, allowing officials of employers and unions to bargain locally.

Albin Taylor and London full-time organiser Joe Burgess represented the union on the national body, which soon agreed on a forty-seven hour week, twelve days annual holiday and payment of overtime at enhanced rates. It wouldn't, however, move on the union's central demand that a national wage rate should be established, and this was left for unions and employers to resolve at local level.

Taylor was very enthusiastic about the JICs and believed they had great potential for improving wages and conditions. By 1923 he was telling members that what had been achieved in the short life of the councils would have taken twenty without the negotiation machinery.

Not that the system was without its weaknesses. Chief among these was the failure of many local authorities to affiliate to the councils or recognise their decisions. A survey conducted in 1922 found at least a third of employing authorities not complying with decisions on hours, overtime, holidays and sick pay. A significant number of elected members on councils simply resented the negotiating machinery, insisting they knew how to treat their employees without being told by an outside body. It was also unfortunate that from 1921, when prices began to fall, the sliding scale agreed by the two sides of the councils forced wage levels down. Much of the negotiating, therefore, in these early years, was concerned with the scale of the cuts. Without doubt they were less draconian than occurred in the private sector, but the wage levels were generally lower in the public services, so any cut had severe effects on living standards.

Although membership inevitably fell away

in these difficult years, Taylor's recruitment methods were as aggressive as ever, and in 1920 he took the union into Birmingham. This brought the National Union of General Workers (formerly Gas Workers Union) out fighting, and in particular they questioned Taylor's tactics in employing as a recruiter an ex-General Workers branch secretary, who had been found guilty of mishandling union funds. Consequently the NUCW were excluded from the West Midlands JIC in 1921. Taylor took the issue to the TUC Disputes Committee, who ruled that the NUCW should be reinstated, only to have the decision over-ruled by the general council.

Taylor also clashed with powerful interests inside the Corporation Workers, most notably over the appointment of full-time officials. One of the union's most able branch secretaries and Executive members, Tom McGrath, had been appointed as Assistant General Secretary in 1918, only to die tragically in 1921. Taylor believed there was not enough work to justify a replacement for McGrath, claiming the JICs had taken much of the negotiating work away. He resisted pressure from the London branches for an appointment and the matter was only settled at annual conference in July 1922, on a card vote of 137 to 119 in Taylor's favour. Taylor's view prevailed, but not without division and resentment.

A similar dispute followed with the Scottish activists, who insisted that the 1600 membership in Edinburgh justified a full-time organiser. Once again Taylor resisted, but on this occasion the Executive over-ruled the General Secretary and appointed Michael Carabine as Scottish District Secretary in 1924.

Within a few months the Edinburgh branch were involved in a skirmish with the Town Council over a comprehensive claim covering all departments. The union gave notice of intention to call a strike, only to be met by a counter-threat that if they did come out they would be dismissed, and workers in the gas, electricity and water departments would risk imprisonment under the 1875 Conspiracy and Protection of Property Act. Taylor, Carabine and the Edinburgh branch were shocked by this response and immediately withdrew the strike notice. Negotiations covering non-trading staff opened again and

the union, in the end, accepted a minimum wage of fifty-three shillings.

TAYLOR RETIRES

During the Edinburgh dispute Taylor asked the Executive Council to consider his retirement on grounds of age, ill health and dissatisfaction. In one sense this request surprised the Executive, because he was only fifty-eight years old and could have served the union until 1931. He had expressed no previous desire to retire early and the Executive detected no slacking off in his work rate. In another sense, perhaps they were not so surprised. On a number of important issues the General Secretary had been out of step with his Ex-

There was always tremendous rivalry between the unions trying to organise municipal employees in Bristol. After setting up a number of branches in 1908 and appointing a full-time official, Alfred Ellery, a series of defections took place leaving a solitary branch which had been with the MEA and Corporation Workers since 1900.

National Union of Corporation Workers,

Registered No. 1386 T.

Affiliated to Trades' Union Congress, Local Trades' Councils, Labour Parties, etc., and represented on Industrial Councils for Local Authorities, etc.

Offices—

138 FIRST AVENUE, LONDON, E.12

PHONE—ILFORD 127

President—
Councillor S. SMITH.

Secretary—
Mr. A. TAYLOR.

*Organiser—***Mr. J. BURGESS.**

To celebrate the Coming-of-Age (21 to-day) of the BRISTOL BRANCH

AND TO

OPEN A NEW BRANCH ROOM,

A Mass Meeting

of Bristol Corporation Workers

WILL TAKE PLACE ON

Saturday, Sept. 10th, 1921,

AT 7 P.M, AT THE

"DUKE OF DEVONSHIRE"

TEMPLE STREET.

Chairman - Alderman F. L. BROWN,

SUPPORTED BY

Alderman H. ANSTEY and A. TAYLOR, Gen. Secretary, with local Officials.

ALL COME ! UNITY IS STRENGTH.

A. TAYLOR, Secretary.

(P.T.O.)

National Union of Corporation Workers,

Registered No. 1386 T.

Affiliated to Trades' Union Congress, Local Trades' Councils, Labour Parties, etc., and represented on Industrial Councils for Local Authorities, etc.

Offices—

138 FIRST AVENUE, LONDON, E.12

PHONE—ILFORD 127.

President—
Councillor S. SMITH.

Secretary—
Mr. A. TAYLOR.

*Organiser—***Mr. J. BURGESS.**

Re suggested Appointment of District Secretary for Edinburgh.

In view of the demand, by some members, for above, in Edinburgh, and the recent meetings and Ballot on same, your Executive Council feel the members cannot fully appreciate the gravity of such a step. The recent Ballot was, in our opinion, inconclusive, many members not voting; your E.C., therefore, have directed another Ballot. They do not admit the right of any branch to a paid official; such must be determined after review of the whole Union For instance—this claim of Edinburgh with 1,600 members—if that right was admitted, any other district with 1,600 could claim the same and so on. In that way all the contributions would go to *officials.*

Assuming an official had been on the last six years the figures would work out (taking the income to Head Office and expenses of 1915-1920) thus :—

Income to Head Office for the six years, £3946 ; Funeral Claims, Accident Benefit, General Secretary's Visits, etc., £802 ; placed to Reserve Funds, £3144.

Wages and Expenses of an Official, say £400 per annum, £2,440 ; leaving £744, or only £150 per annum to the good.

What good would that be to fight the City Council with ?

Other arguments advanced are :—

a That your money comes to London. So it does, but placed to the Reserve Funds of the Union, and is still yours, in common with members in other parts of the country, and your delegates on the Executive Committee and Annual Conference helps to control it, and

The Bethnal Green branch was always one of the strongest in the union. This sash was worn by the branch secretary at demonstrations.

The Edinburgh branch was easily the largest in the union in 1921 with 1600 members spread across the Corporation's departments. Not surprisingly the activists demanded a full-time officer. Taylor resisted but was forced to concede in 1924 when a lamp-lighter, Michael Carabine, was employed.

ecutive. In 1919 they opposed his decision to stand in the East Ham Council election against the Labour candidate because he had been de-selected. The Executive subsequently changed this decision, but must have been uncomfortable backing a 'real labour candidate' against the official candidate. During the dispute about the replacement Assistant General Secretary, Taylor alleged that members of the Executive were up to no good, manoeuvring behind his back. And then, over the appointment of the Scottish District Secretary, the Executive asserted their right to decide how the union should be organised.

Taylor clearly had a very strong view about how he wanted the union to develop, but it was not always accepted by the Executive or the wider union membership as expressed at national conference. He assumed that his vast experience and proud record would persuade others to take his view, but this was not always the case. Many members had joined the Corporation Workers in recent years and knew nothing – except perhaps through folklore – of the MEA dispute. The emotional bonds which bound together Taylor and the dissidents from London in 1907 were loosening, and with this his idiosyncrasies were becoming less understood.

Taylor himself knew that the Corporation Workers were facing difficult times ahead, especially with the competition of the general unions, now lined up in powerful amalgamations. They now included the MEA which had helped to establish the General and Municipal Workers Union in 1924. Taylor had served municipal workers for over twenty years and made a unique contribution through the formative and turbulent years. The challenge of building a strong union for all grades of municipal workers he now passed on to another.

4. NUPE takes shape
1925-33

JACK WILLS TAKES OVER

Although Albin Taylor's request for early retirement was submitted in the summer of 1924, it was not until August 1925 that the Executive Council appointed his replacement, Jack Wills, a London building workers' leader and municipal labour politician.

Born in Poplar in 1877, Jack Wills had found his way into trade union activity through the Operative Bricklayers Society in the late 1890s. By 1914 he was involved in the agitation which led to a building workers 'lock-out' – an experience which helped confirm his belief in an industrial union for all building workers. He became secretary of the Building Workers Industrial Union in August 1914, a position he retained until joining the Corporation Workers in 1925.

His militant trade unionism was accompanied by a close involvement in local government politics in his adopted home of Bermondsey, where he became Labour's first Alderman in 1909. Naturally he took a close interest in labour questions and formed a close association with the strong Corporation Workers Union branches for manual, clerical and poor law workers. He therefore had considerable experience of the concerns facing local authority workers when he took over as General Secretary in October 1925.

One of these issues, the attack on a number of Labour councils because of their wage policies, he knew from personal experience. Bermondsey, like Bethnal Green, Battersea, Stepney, Woolwich and Poplar Councils had come under strong pressure to reduce minimum wage levels set above the Metropolitan JIC level. The four pounds minimum paid by Poplar was brought to the attention of the District Auditor, who decided that it was an excessive payment. The Council appealed against the decision and in 1925 the case

Jack Wills, General Secretary 1925-33.

In the aftermath of the general strike, trade union organisation became very difficult, as London Organiser Joe Burgess reported to the Executive Council, in October 1926:

❝ Since the general strike it is very hard to try and organise men or women. You get insulted and bullied, but in spite of that and the opposition I meet from rivals of other unions, I claim that we as a union are more than holding our own. ❞

A press report of a Corporation Workers meeting. Wood Green Sentinel, 21 January 1926.

went to the House of Lords, who ruled that the minimum was unreasonable and should be reduced. The District Auditor then turned his attention to other authorities who paid above the JIC rate and one by one they were forced to reduce wages to the negotiated sum plus a small concession of 10 per cent.

Jack Wills was closely involved in these de-bates, defending the right of elected public representatives to enter in agreements with trade unions without interference from 'un-elected public officials'. By now NUPE was back in the TUC and Labour Party, and Wills was able to put the Corporation Workers' case to the movement. At the 1927 TUC del-egates backed a call for a protest to the Min-istry of Health. Wills subsequently led the TUC deputation to the Minister, but by this time the Government were progressing legis-lation to strengthen the position of the Dis-trict Auditor.

By the 1929 TUC, the union was hoping that the recently elected Labour government would repeal the measure, and in his speech to Congress Wills reminded delegates what the new Labour Minister for Health, Arthur Greenwood, had said when the legislation was passing through parliament:

> we on this side cannot escape from the conclusion that this Bill is a studied attempt to suppress either local authorities or public authorities with whose political views they do not agree.

When a trade union delegation, including Wills, met Greenwood, they were told that, al-though the Minister was sympathetic to re-moving the legislation, parliamentary time would not allow it.

THE GENERAL STRIKE

Wage-cutting was the familiar response to economic crises and it was this policy which led to a major confrontation between the trade unions and the employers, backed by the government, in 1926. The general strike arose out of the TUC's commitment to de-fend the miners 'locked-out' by the coal own-ers, who were determined to cut pay and eliminate the guaranteed minimum standard wage. A nationwide stoppage of work from 4 May was called by the TUC who assumed full control of the strike.

Some members of the NUCW were called on strike on 5 May when the General Coun-cil instructed all work on road maintenance to cease. Two days later members in electric-ity supply were called out. By now the strike was growing and, with communication diffi-cult, members of the union sometimes re-sponded to strike calls by local committees, rather than instructions from head office.

Wills was able to get across the seriousness of the situation in circulars advising members to beware of 'persons inciting workers to attack or riot... Beware of persons who may be engaged to act as spies and to induce Trade Unionists to create disorder... Take no notice of anything said on the wireless as it is under the control of government.' Another circular stressed the need to maintain union strength during the strike: 'if we allow our organisation to weaken as a result of this dispute, goodness only knows what will happen to our conditions after the dispute is settled.'

As the strike gathered momentum a small group of trade union leaders – excluding miners leaders – were involved in discussions with coal owners and government representatives, which led to the strike being called off on 12 May. The negotiations extracted no serious concessions from the coal owners and the miners were left to fight alone. Wills and the Executive of the Corporation Workers were as stunned as anyone at the conclusion of the strike, and the union continued to support the miners with large donations which pushed the finances into the red.

The extent of sympathetic action in support of the miners infuriated establishment figures and institutions who called on the government to prevent it happening again. Typical of these was the influential *Municipal Journal* which in October 1926 asked:

> What is the relation between the public employee and the rest of the community? Because of his sympathy with the demands of workmen in private employment, shall he be free to cut off the gas, water and electricity supplies, stop passenger transport, leave the sewers to be choked and the towns refuse undestroyed? Are public services to be suspended as that fever can supplement an aborted misuse of trade unionism?

The government had already made up its mind about these issues and its conclusions were embodied in the Trades Disputes Act, which became law in 1927. Workers in essential public services were prohibited from taking strike action and faced heavy fines or imprisonment should they disobey the law.

Faced with these repressive measures, Jack Wills was aware of the need to tighten up the

The Price of Toryism

NOTICE
ALL WAGES REDUCED
BY ORDER OF
THE **TORY GOVERNMENT**

BERMONDSEY BOROUGH COUNCIL

PAY OFFICE

The Wages of Council Workmen are ordered to be cut forthwith.

* * *

YOUR TURN NEXT

union's organisation so it could survive the difficult times ahead. Branches were instructed to step up recruitment, ensure that accounts were kept up-to-date and maintain contact with members. Area conferences and District Committees were set up in 1927, bringing together secretaries and chairmen to discuss vital negotiating issues and provide a link between the branch and Executive Council. A new head office was purchased in 1927 at Blackheath and from here two new organisers, Arthur Moyle and George Cathpole, were to work. All the changes cost money, but Wills was able to convince the Executive that it should be seen as an investment that would return an improved and larger organisation.

NUCW BECOMES NUPE

Wills was also conscious of proposed legislation that would reform local government,

As a Bermondsey councillor and General Secretary of the Corporation Workers, Jack Wills was closely involved in the attempt to resist wage cuts imposed by the District Auditor. The left wing inside the Labour Party wanted the Councils to defy the government and refuse to implement the cuts. Wills had some sympathy with this position but recognised that ultimately a change in law would require a change of government. After successfully proposing a resolution at the 1926 TUC calling on the movement to protest against the surcharging of councillors refusing to make wage cuts, he was a member of the TUC delegation to the Minister, Neville Chamberlain. Cartoon from Bermondsey Labour Magazine, July 1927.

including one changing the name to the National Union of Public Employees (NUPE).

While Jack Wills was undoubtedly correct in seeing the potential of the Local Government Act of 1929, he probably didn't anticipate the extra work it brought to NUPE. Hundreds of individual problems arose as staff were transferred and each had to be patiently pursued with the authority – some of whom employed labour on worse conditions than the staff were expecting. On superannuation rights, for instance, many local authorities had no scheme for manual staff transferring existing pension rights.

The London County Council carried forward its poor record on labour issues by insisting that hundreds of transferred staff from Labour controlled Boards of Guardians take cuts in wages of between two and thirty shillings. Following this decision, Jack Wills was prompted to advise the LCC leader Sir William Ray and his supporters

> that their repressive rule has done more to quicken the political consciousness of the transferred staff than fifty years of Labour propaganda could have done and they can rest assured that at the next LCC elections of 1934, we shall do our utmost to see to it that Labour will be returned to County Hall with a bumping majority.

Arthur Hall joined the MEA in Woolwich in 1901 and quickly became secretary of one of the biggest branches of the union. He served on the Executive Council for many years and became President of NUPE in 1929.

bringing poor law administration under county and borough council control. County councils in particular were a neglected area of trade union activity and Wills proposed that the union set about organising them. To do this, he argued, the union needed a new approach and new name – one that was more embracing. A special conference was held in London on 19 August 1928 at which these proposals were endorsed by delegates,

The publicity attracted by NUPE in defence of transferred officers encouraged a group of members of the National Union of County Officers in South Wales to approach Wills seeking possible membership. Many of these former poor law employees were highly political – living in a part of Wales associated with intense industrial struggle and Labour controlled authorities. Their former employ-

---

The National Government elected in October 1931 encouraged employers, including local authorities, to cut wages. W C Broughton, of the Nottingham General Branch of NUPE, criticised this policy because it would only make a bad situation worse:

❛ To suppose that a general reduction of wages in National, Municipal and other services would be of any assistance to the industrial problem of today is a gross and serious mistake. For it is obvious that with reduced wages it would mean that the wage-earning masses would have a reduced spending power, and this would result in a general falling off of trade. ❜

ers, the Boards of Guardians, had been criticised by the government for their solidarity with workers in times of struggle and adversity. And the employees were now looking to play their part in the work of the wider trade union and labour movement, which they had been unable to do in National Union of County Officers as it was not affiliated to the TUC or Labour Party. An arrangement was made and in early 1932 new branches of NUPE were established in Merthyr, Aberdare, Pontypridd, Llywnpia and Bridgend. The former County Officers organiser Jack Adkin was taken on to the staff and a seat on the Executive secured for the leading lay member Richard Jones from Merthyr. With branches quickly opening up in Neath, Cardiff and the Rhondda, NUPE applied for recognition to the Glamorgan County Council, but found all the seats on the trade union side of the advisory committee taken by NALGO who refused to give any ground.

Representation on negotiating bodies was also a major concern of the union in the on-going dispute with the East and West Midlands JICs. In an attempt to break the log-jam, Wills appealed directly to Will Thorne, general secretary of the General and Municipal Workers, who was satisfied that the exclusion of NUPE was justified. Wills raised the matter again with the TUC Disputes Committee in 1930, putting the case this time that one of the chief functions of the TUC was to uphold collective bargaining which was being denied to a significant number of workers. The Committee were not swayed by these arguments and stood by the General Council decision of 1923 that the TUC had no power to determine representation on JICs. Wills and the Executive recognised that they had come to a dead-end and seriously considered a libel case against the General Workers.

On the remaining JICs where NUPE was represented, relations with the General Workers were amicable. Agreement was reached on who held the secretary and chair-

As staff were transferred from Boards of Guardians to County Councils following the 1929 Local Government Act, NUPE organised and lobbied to ensure that wages and conditions were not undermined. A particular concern was superannuation.

A
Mass Meeting
OF
POOR LAW WORKERS
WILL BE HELD AT
MEMORIAL HALL,
FARRINGDON STREET, LONDON, E.C.
ON
TUESDAY, NOV. 12, 1929,
WHEN
J. V. WILLS
(*General Secretary*)
WILL EXPLAIN
THE SUPERANNUATION PROPOSALS
OF THE
LONDON COUNTY COUNCIL
FOR
POOR LAW EMPLOYEES.

Chair will be taken at 7.0 p.m. by
Councillor I. STOKES
(*Bermondsey Poor Law Branch*)
SUPPORTED BY
Members of the London County Council, Boards of Guardians, and Borough Councils.

This question affects the interest of every Poor Law Worker, High Paid or Low Paid, Male or Female.

If you are desirous of protecting your future welfare, you will not fail to attend.

You cannot afford to be absent.

Charles Agomber, President in 1930-1. He was also a Labour Councillor in his native Bethnal Green during the 1920s.

ployers threatened to suspend meetings of the Council unless this new condition was accepted, but the unions were not going to be bullied and eventually they won their case and the proposal was dropped.

LEAN YEARS

By the summer of 1931, employers were looking again at wage reductions as a solution to the economic crisis facing the country. The Labour government were being advised to make public expenditure cuts to balance its accounts. Amid fears that unemployment had reached dangerous proportions at 2.5 million, and unable to reach agreement about a recovery programme, the Labour Cabinet resigned, only for Ramsay Macdonald – the former Labour Prime Minister – to emerge the next day as Prime Minister of a National Government including Conservatives and Liberals. The National Government had no hesitation in stepping up the programme of cuts which soon began to bite in the local government sector.

man's positions on the trade union side, what the negotiating objectives were and how the arguments would be deployed in support of the claim. They also consistently encouraged the employers' side to seek additional affiliations from backward local authorities and protested when authorities withdrew because they weren't prepared to pay the going rate. The unions also stood together in 1930 in opposition to a move at the National JIC by the employers to prevent unions submitting individual claims to affiliated authorities. The em-

Local authorities were encouraged to cut wages by organisations such as the National Ratepayers Association, who portrayed the municipal workers as a pampered and favoured group – not exposed to the realities of competition. Many authorities didn't need any encouragement to cut wages, threatening employees with dismissal if they were not prepared to accept the new conditions. Some reductions were made on the sliding scale based on the cost of living index which had been falling since 1927. NUPE objected to the use of this index as a basis for wage reductions because it assumed an outdated pattern of expenditure. Wills in 1932 was able to point to a 54 per cent increase in rents since 1914 when the index was drawn up, which

Walter Conquer had been President of the union in 1915-7 and remained as a Trustee for many years after leaving the Executive Council. He composed many rhymes for the Journal including this example from 1932 using the letters NUPE:

> ❛ Numerous benefits to members by our rules we give;
> Universal advance to make life fit to live;
> Progress our motto, good wages we claim,
> Enthusiasm by all will accomplish our aim. ❜

had not been taken into account in the calculations: 'When wages are reduced and the working man has to economise, he cannot economise in rent. He must have shelter for himself and his family.' He went on to question the basis of the comparison with 1914, 'irrespective of whether such a standard was adequate or not. Are we to be riveted to the pre-war standard for ever?'

One authority who would have answered Jack Wills in the affirmative, was Fulham Borough Council, who in 1932 canvassed support for a plan which would have cut sick and holiday pay, and overturned the metropolitan JIC decisions to respect better conditions where they prevailed. The council argued that the workers were being 'spoon fed' which was bad for the rate-payer and bad for the men. Fulham also quoted the inferior terms and conditions prevailing under the agreement of the Public Workers' Conciliation Board – comprised of public works contractors and trade unions – and suggested they be adopted for manual workers.

Proposals for draconian reductions in wages and conditions frequently surfaced as municipal elections came around and candidates attempted to prove their cost-cutting credentials to the voters. Jack Wills was conscious of the disadvantage of his members' wages and conditions being in the public spotlight as he made clear in 1932:

> the municipal worker becomes a shuttle cock. First one has a pitch, then another, at the present time everyone seems to be having a tilt. First a dart is thrown at his wages, then at his overtime, then his holidays, then his sick pay, and then his superannuation. The mere fact that his wages are paid from the rates seems sufficient justification for every Tom, Dick and Harry to join in the attack.

Inevitably these were also lean years for the union as membership stagnated at around 13,000 and the finances slipped into the red. The 1932 conference considered the plight of the union and made a number of changes aimed at reducing expenditure, including a rationalisation of death benefits. It also asked the Executive to consider in detail the situation and make recommendations to the next conference.

NOTES ON SCOTTISH AFFAIRS.

The savage attack on wages still continues in the sacred name of economy. Fife County Council have reduced wages and salaries by 7 per cent., and we are handicapped in our efforts here on behalf of our members by the fact that the employees are scattered all over the county, and are badly organised as a result. Many of these men had agreed to the reduction while we were negotiating, in the belief that if they did not do so, that dismissal was the alternative. We were instrumental, however, in securing that no wage would be reduced below 50/- per week. We also lately secured payment of wages during sickness. It would pay the non-union employees of the County Council to join up with us. The local Secretary is **George Stenhouse, Cartmore Road, Lochgelly.**

The success of the wage settlement in Edinburgh, negotiated by our Union, is becoming more emphasised every day. Glasgow employees, catered for by another Union, are faced with a reduction of 4/- per week on a wage of 55/- (in Edinburgh the reduction on 55/- is 1/6), and, in addition, holidays with pay are to be reduced from 12 days to 8 days. These recommendations of the wages and salaries committee have still to be approved by the Corporation.

The influence of our Union is increasing in Edinburgh and district, and many reforms and wage advances have been secured by us. School Janitors have had their overtime rates increased from 1/6 lit with electricity at our request, in place of paraffin lamps; new cottages are being built to replace out-per evening to 1/3 per hour. Cottages have been of-date ones. An individual workman has had his wages increased from 55/- per week to a scale beginning at 67/- and rising to 71/-. **A feature of our Union is that it gives the same consideration and attention to an individual as to a large number of men.**

Every member of the Union ought to act as an organiser and try and get any non-union men working along with him to join up. The Scottish Organiser is J. M. Airlie, 11, Bonnington Grove, Edinburgh.

The Executive spent some time looking at the options, aware that any increase in basic contributions could have a serious effect on the ability of union to retain and recruit members. Various cost-cutting options were also considered, but they offered little scope as the organisation was already under-resourced in terms of negotiating officers and support staff. In the end the Executive had to recommend an increase of 50 per cent in contributions to six pence a week.

THE DEATH OF JACK WILLS
During these traumatic months, Jack Wills had been in a hospital undergoing major surgery. He carried on as best he could

A report on the union in Scotland from the Journal of March 1932.

sented the report which conference decided to put to a ballot of members.

Following the conference, Jack Wills returned to St. Olave's Hospital in Rotherhithe, where he died on 14 July 1933. His funeral was attended by many old friends from the trade union and socialist movements, including George Hicks representing the TUC and Ben Tillett, the former Transport Union leader.

Those present were reminded of his early involvement in the syndicalist and industrial union movement in the years immediately before and after the war, work which he allied to his intense municipal activity in Bermondsey where he represented Labour as Councillor Alderman and then in 1925 as Mayor. Bermondsey had always been close to NUPE and its predecessor unions, and it was appropriate that the General Secretary should be one of its leading citizens.

The union's President, Bill Setchell, was also a Bermondsey man, so he knew Jack Wills the municipal socialist as well as the trade union General Secretary. Setchell could also testify to the unextinguished fighting spirit of Jack Wills, which surfaced eloquently at the 1932 TUC, despite illness. Seconding a reference back of the TUC General Council's proposals for the management of socialised industries and services to be run by

Harry Catchpole from Ardsley, West Yorkshire, President in 1931-2 and subsequently in 1941-2 and 1948-9.

under the circumstances, rising from his sick bed in June 1933 to attend the special conference considering the Executive's recommendations on the contribution increase. He pre-

---

During 1931, the Labour government faced a deepening economic crisis, and division within its ranks about how it should respond. The Prime Minister, Ramsay MacDonald, accepted the need for spending cuts – including unemployment pay – but he was unable to secure the support of the TUC for this policy. In August he resigned from office and accepted the offer to head a new government with the support of Liberals and Conservatives. Jack Wills, always a socialist militant, saw an inevitability in these events, and a possibility for working class advance, as in his message to members in September, 1931:

❛ Capitalism is rapidly rushing headlong towards its own destruction. It has created a poverty problem which it is totally incapable of curing. Every attempt it makes to cope with the situation only intensifies the problem and adds to its undoing. We are engaged in a struggle as to whether profits and war gains are to be sacrificed or whether the workers are to suffer further wage reductions and the curtailment of social services...

There is no room for pessimism; on the contrary, the movement has been born again. The fire and passion inherent in all human beings to fight against injustice and to protect the downtrodden, which is expressed through the Labour Movement, has been rekindled. The soul of the movement had become sick and anaemic. The battle has called forth new blood and re-invigoration. Unity of purpose, faith in our principles, determination in resistance, honour to those who have remained steadfast, will bring renewed strength and ultimate victory. ❜

'people appointed by the government solely on the grounds of their fitness for the position', Wills had said that all they were proposing was a

> glorified Whitley Council... The time has arrived when we want something more... the sooner the Congress sets in earnest about the task of devising ways and means whereby we can control industry, the better it will be for the working class movement. The General Council suggests a slide whereby capitalism can comfortably slip into socialism, but instead of providing a slide they have put up a prop which, if we are not very careful, will maintain capitalism for many years.

When he took over in 1925, Jack Wills found a trade union built largely around the personality of the former General Secretary. He made important organisational improvements – including the introduction of area conferences and the expansion of the organising staff. When local government re-organisation was proposed, he understood the importance of broadening the union's image and name to take advantage of new possibilities, and finally, when the union run into deficit, he proposed solutions which he knew were necessary if unpopular. By laying down the conditions for financial security, Jack Wills had helped open up the next phase in NUPE's development.

Digging up the road with pneumatic drills at the Cenotaph in Whitehall, c 1933.

5. Expansion
1934-48

NUPE's delegation to the 1934 TUC. Left to right: Bryn Roberts, Richard Jones and David Stephen.

THE APPOINTMENT OF BRYN ROBERTS

Following Jack Wills's death, the national organiser based at the Blackheath office, Arthur Moyle, took over much of the day-to-day work of running the union, in co-operation with the President, Bill Setchell and the Lady Clerk, Flo Fancett.

Within days of burying Wills, a letter was received from Will Thorne, the general secretary of the General and Municipal Workers Union, inviting discussions about a possible amalgamation. The matter was put before the Executive at the end of July, but following the meeting Setchell wrote to Thorne advising him that because of the stress caused by the death of the general secretary it was not possible to give proper attention to the matter and it was not raised again.

Finding a new general secretary became urgent and by the first week in December candidates were being interviewed, among them a young miners' official from South Wales who stood out so clearly that the Executive did not hesitate in appointing him.

A press report from the Whitby Gazette of 18 December 1936 of a NUPE branch meeting at which the organiser, Wilson Coates, gave details of the union's claims for improvements in wages and conditions.

Bryn Roberts was only thirty-six years old, but he had acquired experience in all aspects of the labour movement and the breadth of his activity impressed the Executive.

As a boy working in the Pennybont pit in Abertillery he had been caught up in strikes and became deeply influenced by the self-improving traditions of the miners – attending classes in industrial history and economics. By the time he was called up to serve in the war, he had developed a class consciousness which gave him the strength to resist conscription resulting in a prison sentence which he served until the war ended in 1918.

In January 1920 he went to London to study at the marxist Central Labour College where among his contemporaries were Aneurin Bevan, Ted Williams and James Griffiths – all to become prominent Labour Members of Parliament in later years. After distinguishing himself at the Labour College, Roberts returned to Abertillery and was soon elected to important positions within the South Wales Miners Federation, first as checkweighman and then in 1926 as agent and secretary of the Rhymney Valley District. To his considerable negotiating experience, he added political responsibility when elec-

ted to the Rhymney District Council in 1926.

Bryn Roberts had all the qualities and experience the executive were looking for, and he duly began work at the head office in the first week of 1934.

One of his first duties was to receive a deputation from a London branch who were to submit a motion to the forthcoming national conference, calling on the Executive to approach the General and Municipal Workers for amalgamation talks – following Thorne's request in July.

There was a view developing within a number of branches that with only 13,000 members NUPE could not survive against the competition of the giant general workers' unions. Roberts listened to the arguments and explained to the members that he had bold plans involving a major recruitment exercise, based initially in London but soon stretching out to unorganised workers all over the country. The delegation were convinced of these plans and the motion never appeared at conference.

PLANS FOR EXPANSION

The ideas Roberts alluded to were set out in a coherent and comprehensive paper submitted to the Executive at their April meet-

ing. Three questions were posed:

1. Can the Union survive indefinitely on its present limited personnel?
2. Will it ultimately be submerged by competing trade union forces?
3. Will elements within NUPE successfully advocate amalgamating voluntarily with the NUGMW or TGWU?

To these questions, Roberts replied, 'the danger of extinction, voluntarily or otherwise, is greater if the union stands still than would be the risk of failure if an ambitious programme of expansion were embarked upon.' This expansion programme would involve the appointment of more full-time officers who would act initially as recruiters. Roberts believed that in the first phase of expansion, these organisers should be based in London because of the high concentration of unorganised workers and the possibilities of success following the recent local government elections which saw Labour returned as the majority party on the LCC. The shorter travelling distances in London would also mean that the new appointments were likely to be more economical in recruitment terms than would provincial appointments, where more

Formal dinner at the 1936 NUPE Conference in London.

travelling would be involved.

Roberts was aware that any expansion involving additional expenditure on an unsure financial position involved risks. Indeed he recognised that:

> few business houses would take such a risk. However, we are backing our fancy not in a fatalistic way, but in the knowledge as far as it is ascertainable, that this union has a unique opportunity, which if now grasped, will lead onto success – but if not grasped will in my own

view, be likely to lead to death and decay.

With Executive backing, Roberts was able to attend his first national conference – aptly held in Cardiff – in May 1934 and present in outline form his proposals for expansion. Delegates wholeheartedly supported these plans as they too felt the need for the union to step up its activities.

The President, Bill Setchell, was also able to give the delegates the good news that membership was holding up following the re-

Outside of the South Wales coalfield Bryn Roberts was not well known, so when he was appointed to NUPE in December 1933, members were unaware of the sort of man who had become general secretary. One of these members, Ted Robinson, who went onto become an organiser for the union, describes his first impressions of Roberts at the North West Area Conference of March 1934 in the Clarion Club, Market Street, Manchester.

❜ He was a stranger to us all when Conference opened we were wondering what sort of fellow he would turn out to be. We had little doubts when he concluded his speech, in which he not only revealed a remarkable knowledge of local government problems but also offered remedies most likely to solve them… (he) enunciated for the first time the principles for a national wage policy for county roadmen and other sections of local government. He also outlined what our organisational policy should be, and to the delegates he gave the union an unmistakable purpose which not only commanded the enthusiastic support of those present but was also to command the support of the entire membership. ❜

NUPE believed the case for a national rate for county road-workers was unanswerable.

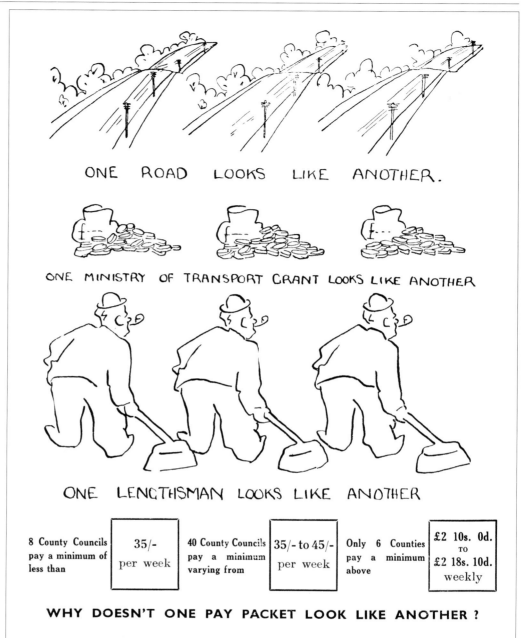

cent increase in contributions, providing 'the complete answer to those who sought to discredit our organisation by stating that our members only retained their membership because it was cheap.'

Against this background, the Executive were soon able to proceed with the first stage of the plan and by January 1935, two new organisers were in place working in the London area under the general secretary's instructions that, 'I want you to realise that you must not fail; that everyone of us must constantly be on our toes to put the job through.' The new organisers took this advice to heart and within a year had increased the membership in London by more than 50

per cent to over 12,000.

With the expansion plan proving itself in London, Roberts was able to go to the Executive in early 1935 with suggestions for further appointments. Outside the capital there were only three organisers – Bob Bury, a national officer based in Nottingham, Jack Airlie in Edinburgh and Jack Adkin in Wales. Bury, in particular, had an enormous patch to cover, stretching from Yorkshire to Worcestershire. This burden was relieved when the Executive agreed to new appointments in Yorkshire, the West Midlands and the North West.

NUPE organisation in the North-West area in 1934 was confined to small branches in

St.Helens, Crewe, Rochdale, Bootle and Burnley, and a new branch at Nantwich had opened up in the summer based exclusively on the roadmen employed by Cheshire County Council. These men worked under miserable conditions earning, in some cases, as little as thirty-seven shillings for a forty-eight hour week. The officer appointed for the North West in 1935, Ted Robinson, saw the potential for organisation amongst these workers and set about winning them to NUPE. By the autumn he was reporting 'really remarkable progress', with fifteen branches opened in Cheshire for county road workers bringing together 1,750 members – nearly all the men employed.

ORGANISING THE ROAD WORKERS

Ted Robinson's success didn't go unnoticed at head office. Bryn Roberts quickly took up the idea of NUPE becoming the county road-workers' union and pushed it among the organisers, who were encouraged to go out into the county to find gangs of roadmen and talk to them about the benefits of joining NUPE.

What the organisers found were thousands of appallingly paid and treated workers who had been neglected by the trade union move-

ment but who were willing to join NUPE when persuaded that it could lead to improvements.

Wages in the counties of the North and East Riding of Yorkshire in 1936 were among the lowest, at thirty-three shillings for fifty hours work. This wage is put into perspective when it is considered that the social investigator Seebohm Rowntree had calculated that in 1935 a minimum of fifty-one shillings and three pence was necessary to keep a family of five out of poverty. Roadworkers were not paid for holidays or when it was wet and they were unable to work, nor did they receive any enhanced rates for overtime. The working conditions were also abysmal as one roadman related in a letter to a Hull newspaper in 1937:

We have to ride miles to work and be there by 7.00 am, and we have to carry our tools on our cycles, which we have to keep in repair and get no allowance. A roadman has to do a lot of different jobs – bricklayer's and joiner's work as well as concreting, spreading tarmac, setting curbs and draining, and has to endure the tortures of the tar-spraying for which he receives 6d a day extra. No goggles are provided and a suit of clothes, underclothing and boots are

Members of the Watford branch on the 1938 May Day demonstration.

National Union of General and Municipal Workers
Transport and General Workers' Union
National Union of Public Employees

Members of either of the above Unions, employed by local
authorities, are invited to attend a

MASS MEETING

in the

Memorial Hall
Farringdon Street, E.C.

on

TUESDAY, JUNE 14th, 1938

at **7.30** p.m.

when a report on their recent J.I.C. efforts to secure an increase
of wages for Council employees will be given by—

G. DEIGHTON, N.U.G.M.W.
A. MOYLE, N.U.P.E.
S. PECK, T. & G.W.U.

Chair to be taken by J. EDWARDS, N.U.G.M.W.

Admission only by Trade Union Ticket

Watford Printers Limited (T.U.), 58 Vicarage Road, Watford.   9188

*In spite of differences, NUPE was
able to work with the general
unions in campaigning for a pay
increase from the LCC in 1938.*

ruined every year.

No shelters are provided. When away from
home we get our dinners behind a hedge or
go into farm buildings if there are any handy.

Is it any wonder that 95 per cent of us have
joined the National Union of Public Employers to try and better pay and conditions?

The majority of county councils were dominated by wealthy employers, farmers, land-
owners and retired army officers – hardly a
recipe for good employment practices – and
frequently the vested interests of members

would come to the fore when wages and conditions of county employees were being discussed. Farmers in particular disliked NUPE
submitting claims for improvements for roadworkers, whom they preferred to keep on a
level with their own farmworkers. Indeed the
casual nature of much road work was perpet-
uated by employers who favoured a pool of
labour being available for work on the farms
when it was necessary.

Where the union recruited roadmen it
would study their conditions and prepare a
claim for improvements based usually on a
minimum wage of fifty shillings and eleven
pence for a forty-seven hour week, with demands for sick and holiday pay. The claim
was always well researched and presented, detailing the increasing cost of living, evidence
from the British Medical Association showing
how poverty affected health, and comparative statistics of wages in surrounding areas
and industries. The claim would be sent to
the national and local press and in many
cases received extensive and sympathetic coverage, helping to apply pressure on county
councillors, whose labour policies were increasingly becoming a matter of public debate. Frequently the council commented that
the claim from NUPE was the first it had received from a trade union. Typically small
concessions were made – such as half a
penny on the hourly rate, moving it a stage
closer to the union's minimum of one shilling and a penny.

This was how progress was made in the
North and East Ridings of Yorkshire, where
successive improvements in 1936 and 1937
gave increases of nearly ten shillings, equivalent to twenty per cent of the basic wage. In
the following year North Riding were forced
to guarantee a forty-eight hour week – irrespective of weather – holiday pay, and the
placing of all permanent men on the superannuation scheme. Roadmen flooded into
the branches following these successes and
the union prepared for the next claim
stronger than it had been before.

As membership continued to grow (it
reached 33,000 by early 1937), particularly in
rural areas among county roadmen, Bryn
Roberts detected an organisational weakness,
which could if left unchecked, stifle the expansion at infancy. The problem arose be-

Public cleansing work in Holborn, London, c 1930.
LONDON BOROUGH OF CAMDEN

cause the new branches were many in number, but individually small in membership, reflecting the scattered nature of the employment. For instance, a branch of the union in Dover might include all the county roadmen employed by Kent County living in the town, but it would probably not number more than one hundred. By 1936, nearly seven out of ten branches had less than one hundred members, and according to Roberts's calculations – which he shared with delegates at the national conference – 'each of these branches, I am sorry to say, is a burden on the organisation. In a word, they constitute a direct loss.' More money was going out of the union's funds to pay for branch commission, administrative costs, full-time officer support and legal and other benefits than was coming in from contributions. Roberts recognised that in the short term, the size of branches would not change, so it was necessary to reduce costs. A comprehensive package of savings was put to the national conference in 1937, which included a reduction of $2^{1}/_{2}$ per

From his very first public speech on behalf of NUPE, Bryn Roberts ran into opposition from the general unions who resented the aggressive intrusion of NUPE and the general secretary's frank and uncompromising stance. In February 1937 Roberts visited Charles Dukes, the general secretary of the General and Municipal Workers, to discuss NUPE's policy on the 40 hour week. Dukes, apparently, wanted an assurance from Roberts that NUPE would not be supporting this demand, because he was resisting such demands from within his union – from the Communist members – and, since the TGWU were also against it, it would not go forwards on the National JIC. In his notes for a report to the Executive, Roberts described this as a 'very regrettable position', and went on:

❛ by such methods the rank and file may lose faith in the present leadership… it strengthened the appeal of the Communists and other outside elements, and endorsed their contention that there was no hope for the workers in the present personnel of the TUC General Council and the national Labour Party. ❜

NUPE's organising work among county council employees included hospital and institutional employees, many working under miserable conditions. In his speech to the 1938 TUC advocating a national wage for county employees, Bryn Roberts said, 'The nurses, the staffs of our Poor Law Institutions and Mental and General Hospitals are also the victims of this higgledy-piggledy method of the independent fixation of hours, wages and conditions, by the sixty-two County authorities. Few institutions operate a 48 hour week. Many impose a working day of 12 to 13 hours. In the County of Surrey there is a town in which there are two institutions. The male staff nurse in the one works fewer hours per week and receives 8s 6d per week more than the male staff nurse in the other, despite the fact that they perform identical duties. It makes me wonder whether the right people are confined inside the institutions.'

National Union of Public Employees

HEAD OFFICE :
8, ABERDEEN TERRACE, BLACKHEATH, LONDON, S.E.3

All Hospital and Institutional Employees of the

WEST RIDING COUNTY COUNCIL

are cordially invited to attend

SPECIAL MEETINGS

(Arranged by kind permission of the Authority)

to be held in the

Wakefield County Institution

on

TUESDAY, 24th MAY, 1938

Commencing at 7 p.m.

Speaker : W. WINDOW

(Area Officer, N.U.P.E.)

Matters affecting the hours, wages and conditions of employment which are being negotiated with the County Council will be under discussion.

Members should make a point of inviting any unorganised employee to attend.

The meeting times have been arranged to allow the opportunity of both day and night shifts to attend, and all grades of employees are asked to make a special effort.

IT PAYS TO ORGANISE

For further particulars apply   -   -   Councillor C. WILDE

C.P.S. (T.U., 44 hours). Tudor St., London, E.C. 4—91984

cent in secretaries' commission, to 10 per cent, biennial conferences to replace the annual conferences with an Executive Council elected for two years, and a minimum number set of 100 members for each branch to be entitled to an automatic conference delegate, doubling the previous figure. Smaller branches would be entitled to an indirect delegate.

In his reply to a lively debate, the general secretary stressed the importance of the changes, without which it would not be possible to make any additional organising appointments, failure to change would 'bring to an end an outstanding trade union achievement.' Conference supported the proposals by nearly two to one and the Executive were able to prepare for the next stage in the expansion plan.

CONFLICT WITH THE GENERAL UNIONS

As new organisers were appointed, they were instructed to recruit in the towns and cities, where concentrations of municipal workers made for cost-effective organisation. Roberts would issue detailed instructions to the organisers, including an assessment of the number of potential recruits in an area and the strength of competitors – particularly the general unions. This strategy inevitably met with resistance from the general unions who in the industrial northern towns and cities were very strong, often with full-time officials sitting as councillors. This was the situation in Darlington and Middlesborough, where NUPE, by 1938, claimed more than half of the non-trading employees in membership, yet still could not get recognition from the local authorities. Roberts alleged that these were under great pressure from the NUGMW not to concede to NUPE. At one point NUPE were considering posting large bills on hoardings informing the public of the failure of the Councils to recognise them, and opening shops in the town centres from which similar information could be distributed. Recognition did eventually come through a working agreement between the two unions at national level in February 1939.

Similar working arrangements were agreed in a number of areas, but conflict was never far below the surface and would frequently emerge as difficult decisions were

made – particularly when the three unions were involved in a dispute with the employer as in London in 1938 and 1939. The dispute had arisen following the failure of London employers – the majority Labour-controlled – to concede an increase necessary to bring their workers up to the level of other areas. The basic rate in London was now only fifty-six shillings which compared very unfavourably with other cities such as Bristol which payed a minimum of sixty-three shillings.

Bryn Roberts was closely involved in the dispute along with Charles Dukes and Ernest Bevin, general secretaries of the General and Municipal Workers Union and Transport and General Workers respectively. Roberts tried unsuccessfully to convince Dukes and Bevin to take a more direct line against the LCC leader Herbert Morrison – 'the acknowledged author of policy ' – and so he took the workers' case to a wider audience through a lavish pamphlet and newspaper articles. Dukes and Bevin took exception to

K. Salembier, from Nottingham, the first woman to be elected to the Executive Council in 1939.

A Bridge is Built : Some of Britain's Roadmen at Work on a New Highway
The road climbs steeply through the woods. One half is open already. The other half must be built up. Where once primroses and bluebells grew, now tons of concrete make a bridge for the road. The concrete mixer and the pneumatic drill make the work possible. But the workman is the vital factor in getting the job done.

A ROADMAN'S DAY

Lengthsmen, labourers, mixers, spreaders, pneumatic-drill operators, screed-layers, curb-layers, skip attendants, asphalt-layers, leading hands—all these are roadmen. All doing a vital war job.

BRITAIN lives by her ocean traffic, but inland communications are also vitally important, most of all in time of war. Not enough is heard of the hundred thousands of men, employees of County Councils, who work day in, day out, in all weathers, to keep the winding roads of England in tip-top condition. Hear Mr. Ernest Short—shrewd, red-faced, twelve years in the Navy and sixteen years a roadman—on the conditions of his trade :

"I work for the Mid-Surrey area. I'm what they call a ganger : that's a foreman, like. There's eight in my gang—nine, counting myself. Mostly we work a forty-eight hour week, or forty-four hours in winter, when the days get very short. You can add on a couple of hours a day for travelling, because a chap may have to bike anything up to twelve miles to and from his work. They pay you for wet time nowadays—didn't used to, before we had the Union— but it's got to be pretty tough weather before we knock off. Of course, the work varies a lot. Asphalting's the

hardest job of all. Why? Because you've got to spread the asphalt while it's still hot, and that means you've got to work quick. My gang, that's nine men, sometimes shift between forty and fifty tons of asphalt in a day. I draw three pounds ten a week, and another four bob war bonus. We're trying for an extra four bob now. Of course, that's a ganger's wage. Some of the others—the engine-driver's mate, for instance—only draw two pound twelve and six, and the bonus. A man has a job to get by on that, these days. But there's been a great improvement all the same. It's not so long back since some of the County Councils were paying as low as thirty-four bob a week, and no holidays or wet time either. The Union's done a lot for us—worth the tanner a week, we always say. Stand it? Oh, yes, I can stand it. It's a healthy life, if you start healthy. But it's kind of tough sometimes, in winter, when you get up on a hog-back road with no cover, and a frozen surface to work on."

There is no doubt that Mr. Short underrates

PICTURE POST

The Man who Makes the Road
The steam-roller is at rest. A roadman pauses to ease his muscles. But the work goes steadily on.

27

what they saw as NUPE's unilateral action, believing it to be typical of Roberts, trying to gain advantage at their expense. Roberts's defence was that nothing had stopped the two general unions from campaigning publicly; but he was aware that what really rankled with them was NUPE's ability to set a pace of activity which they could not compete with. The interests of the general unions extended way beyond the public services and so resources were stretched in many different directions. In contrast NUPE, with its exclusively public service focus, was able to concentrate on issues and give them maximum prominence. Roberts had become an experienced publicist and was aware of the growing importance of the media in projecting the union's message. Well written and researched articles, pamphlets and books poured regularly from the general secretary's office, a testimony to his journalism, hard work, and determination to put NUPE on the map – qualities which made him a formidable opponent.

By the beginning of 1939, Bevin and Dukes were discussing how they could marginalise NUPE, and inevitably their strategy became centred around the general secretary, who they considered should be excluded from the National JIC Executive and Appeals Panel. Roberts got wind of this and wrote to Bevin, asking him if there was any truth in the rumours. Bevin wrote back that Robert's position had indeed been discussed and:

It is true that there has been a general
sickening of the attitude you have adopted to

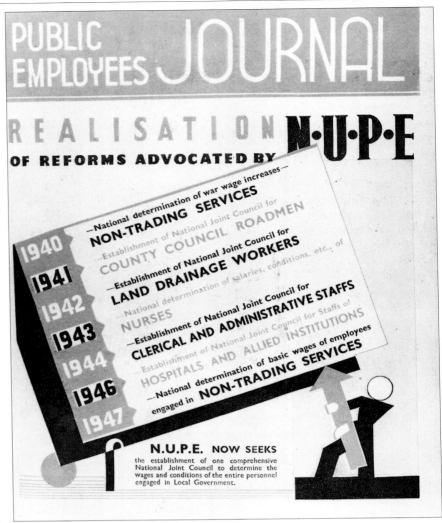

The movement to national wage bargaining in public services.

other unions and that a feeling has grown up that they were not justified in continuing to sit with you.

Bevin accused Roberts of behaving like, 'a bull in a china shop' and asked him to change his ways. If he was able to do so Bevin continued, the representatives on the National JIC would vote for him.

The wages of county roadworkers were well below the fifty-six shillings and sixpence set in 1938 – using the standards set by the social investigator Seebohm Rowntree – as the minimum necessary to keep a family out of poverty. Local authority workers as a whole also compared unfavourably with this minimum standard in 1938, as a contemporary study commented:

❛ Altogether 206,000 workers in the public utility services are earning less than the Rowntree minimum; that is about 55 per cent of all workers covered in the Government survey. If we apply this percentage to the total number of workers employed in these industries we arrive at a figure of 260,000 male workers, almost exclusively employed by Local Authorities, who are paid a weekly wage which cannot keep them fit for work. All the women receive, on the average, weekly earnings below what even Mr Rowntree regards as a minimum. ❜

J Kuczynski, *Hunger and Work*, 1938, p81

Roberts had also fallen out with the general unions at the TUC only a few months earlier in September 1938, when moving NUPE's motion on the establishment of national negotiating machinery for county council workers.

In a masterly speech, Roberts outlined to delegates the chaos of wage determination across sixty-two county authorities.

Take the county road workers' hours. There is no uniformity. The length of the working week is different in over 20 counties. It varies from 47 hours to $52^1/_2$ hours per week.

Wages, which are scandalously low, are in greater variety. The different rates between the 62 County Councils and the differential rates within each, result in hundreds of varying rates of wages being paid for a class of work which is identical in every respect.

Eight County Councils pay minimum wages of less than 35 shillings per week; forty two County Councils pay wages varying from 35 to 45 shillings per week. Only six County Councils pay wages in excess of 50 shillings per week.

The majority of the employees, who are family men, cannot observe the nutritional scale of the British Medical Association nor the Rowntree scale. Their wages are less than the amount they would receive were they in receipt of public assistance or unemployment benefit. These County Councils are the public

health authorities and it is regrettable that they should be responsible for such a scandalous state of affairs.

Roberts also described to delegates the varying conditions of other County Council employees, including nurses and institutional staff, and gave an example of two situations in Guildford, where one institution paid eight shillings and six pence a week more than the other for a staff nurse, 'despite the fact that they perform identical duties. It makes me wonder whether the right people are confined inside the institutions'.

In rejecting joint industrial council arrangements as suitable for County Council staff employees, Roberts said wage levels were determined on a district basis: 'In a depressed area the Joint Industrial Council will reflect distressed conditions; in a rural area, it will reflect agricultural conditions… It is compelled to fix a rate – low of course – most likely to induce the largest number of authorities to become affiliated.'

What was needed, the NUPE general secretary told delegates, was a new national machinery to fix wages, hours and conditions of County Council employees – along the lines of the recently established board for road haulage workers which the TGWU were so pleased with.

The motion was opposed on behalf of the General and Municipal Workers by Mark Hewitson, who said that Bryn Roberts, 'must have sat fishing for a fortnight for the best red herring he could find,' because the National JIC was capable of dealing with county councils' workers' terms and conditions – there was no need for a new body. These views were echoed by Arthur Deakin of TGWU.

In his reply, Roberts criticised the record of the JICs:

> I venture to suggest that those who seek to justify the existing joint industrial council machinery have more courage than wisdom. The Joint Industrial Councils in the Local Government service have existed for 20 years, and during that time five County Councils have been converted to the Joint Industrial Council faith. According to that rate of progress, it will take 230 years to get the other 57 in.

The motion was lost, but Roberts was not one to forget the contents of such an important debate, and at every opportunity he reminded NUPE members that the general unions opposed the establishment of a national negotiating body for county roadworkers.

Alongside the effort to achieve national negotiations for County Council workers, the union was also involved in a big campaign to remove the practice of fortnightly payment by cheque to roadworkers. This practice had developed because it was more convenient for the employers to send a cheque through the post than take out the pay to the men working on the roads; for the roadworkers it was a nightmare, as it meant having to cash the cheque with a local shopkeeper, as this Kent County Council worker related:

> I earn my wages honestly and if the councillors knew of the embarrassment I suffer in changing my wage cheque they would, if they were reasonable men, pay me in cash.
>
> In the village the bank opens one day a week. It is closed when I return from work. My normal practice is to try to get it cashed in the village shop which is normally filled with nosey parkers. Frequently there is not enough money in the till and I am told to come later.
>
> This has distasteful results. On one occasion, a person in the little shop, seeing the cheque and listening to the conversation about changing it, broadcast to the village that I had a good job as she had seen my weekly cheque for £4. It was cruel libel, it was wages for a fortnight.

NUPE approached the Minister of Transport in June 1939, who recognised the grievance and promised to follow it up with the County Councils Association, but nothing was done. The union itself approached the sixty-two councils to end the practice and the matter was referred to the County Councils Association, who again stalled. By the time Roberts met representatives of the Association, he was armed with a legal opinion which confirmed suspicion that payment by cheque was illegal under the Truck Act, which stipulated that wages should be paid in coin of the realm. Roberts made it plain to the representatives that unless they were prepared to issue instructions to counties that they should pay in cash, legal action would be taken. The representatives conceded that the union had the law on their side, but asked for the difficulties created by the out-break of war to be taken into account. Councils were to be asked to meet the unions and reach an agreement in their own area. NUPE was not happy with this and, during the first months of 1940,

---

Having achieved the establishment of a national negotiating body for county roadmen, the unions submitted a claim for a ten shilling increase – lifting the minimum wage to sixty-four shillings – in 1942. It was not enthusiastically received by the employers, and in a widely distributed leaflet Roberts drew a graphic contrast:

❝ The leaders of the County Councils are very distinguished gentlemen. Amongst them are peers of the realm, numerous knights, doctors of law and medicine … I imagine… these and other distinguished county representatives in the comport of their own homes, happily discussing and arranging with their wives the progress of the careers of their sons and daughters … I wonder too, as they argued against granting our 64/- shilling minimum, what happiness existed in the home of the county roadworker. ❞

PUBLIC EMPLOYEES JOURNAL

JULY—AUGUST, 1948

A Message from

THE RT. HON. ANEURIN BEVAN, M.P.

MINISTER OF HEALTH

"Daily Herald" Photograph

Greetings to Members of the National Union of Public Employees. The National Health Service has begun to operate. It provides a complete cover for health for every man, woman and child in this country, without exception, without distinction. The Service completes the full Social Security Scheme. Yet not only does it divorce all forms of health care from ability to pay fees, it also separates the health services from insurance qualification. Everyone, young or old, rich or poor, insured or not, is entitled to all that is available.

This is an Act which will really help the Mothers of Britain. Thank you for all you have done in the fight to get it through. Now let us all work to build the finest health service in the world.

July, 1948.

Cover of the union Journal with a message from the Minister of Health, Aneurin Bevan, announcing the establishment of the National Health Service. Bevan was a close friend of Bryn Roberts.

considered a possible course of action.

Meanwhile recruitment had been hotting up, with branches opening across the counties of Southern England, quickly followed by some negotiating successes. For example, in backward Wiltshire, in July 1939, an increase of two shillings a week was obtained along with a sick pay agreement. This, and agreements like it across the country, were important in that they showed the union was breaking through, securing improvements on a national scale. For the roadworkers concerned, it confirmed their loyalty to NUPE, who had promised them an improvement in their lives if they organised.

The spirit built up by roadworkers in these formative years was captured by Bryn Roberts, when he wrote of the early area conferences:

Although the delegates were all employed by one county authority, they met as perfect

strangers. When they separated, they had cemented bonds of understanding and fellowship which were soon to destroy the ugly individualism that had hitherto characterised their working lives. They became adherents to a new army fashioned to serve a common cause. They were no longer the lonely isolated workers they had been.'

However, the leadership of NUPE were aware that in a significant number of counties – Shropshire, East Sussex, Westmorland, Worcestershire, Devon and Dorset – progress was very slow, and members were becoming dispirited as claim after claim was rejected. Roberts – certainly by the autumn of 1939 – was conscious of the need to make a breakthrough with the campaign for a national negotiating body.

NUPE IN WARTIME

When the war broke out in September, NUPE declared its commitment to get behind the national effort to defeat fascism, by urging its members to continue to carry out their work, which was so important to the country. Branches were advised to expect problems in organising meetings because of the 'black out', and losing members – and particularly active members – to the services.

Roberts, however, was optimistic that NUPE could make progress in these conditions, particularly if Air Raid Precautions staff could be encouraged to join the union. There would also need to be negotiations over a wide range of issues – including a war bonus to compensate for inflation – and much of this would involve direct contact with government officials at a national level. By October, the general secretary went further in a report to the Executive Council, which concluded that the war would create many opportunities, 'and might also be the means of bringing more rapidly to fruition the union national policy on wages and conditions of employment.'

The union had already approached the Ministry of Labour about a number of county councils who refused to negotiate with NUPE, and at a meeting in November Roberts presented the case for the application of the government's Fair Wages Resolution to these authorities. This would oblige these

County Councils – who were acting as contractors for the government in the road building programme – to observe the terms and conditions recognised through collective bargaining in the service.

The union's arguments were obviously persuasive, because on 20 December, a Department of Transport circular advised County Councils that the Fair Wages Resolution did apply to road work and it should be implemented by authorities. The advice also went on to criticise those County Councils who made no attempt to negotiate with the accredited representatives of the unions. The circular commented that in other areas,

> although there is opportunity presented to the unions to state their case, full opportunities for negotiation are not accorded... it has now become common practice for conditions of employment to be freely negotiated between employers and employees and the Minister feels that the general adoption of a similar procedure for road workers would not only be the most satisfactory method of settling conditions of service but would also assist in the maintenance of good relations between highway authorities and their staffs.

This was just the boost the union had been looking for – an endorsement of NUPE's policies – and not surprisingly Bryn Roberts was not slow in letting the world know all about it. Within three weeks a pamphlet telling the story of how NUPE achieved the breakthrough was in circulation. The general unions on the trade union side of the National JIC, at a meeting in March 1940, dissociated themselves from the content of this and a subsequent pamphlet, so reaffirming their opposition to national machinery for County Council workers. As with earlier episodes, the officials of the general unions probably resented the speed with which NUPE was able to respond. Roberts was convinced that 'the implementing of a fair wages clause will inevitably lead to the establishment of our National Wages Board proposal.' He was soon proved right, as Ministry of Transport officials confirmed in a letter of 18 January that... 'the Minister considers if effective machinery is set up for negotiation of conditions of service of roadworkers the complaints which have been made to him by your union and others will be met.'

Clearly the Government supported the establishment of a negotiating body, even if it lacked the drive to bring it about. By early March, Roberts was complaining to the Minister that, contrary to Government advice, Devon County Council were still refusing to meet NUPE representatives. NUPE was looking for a more interventionist approach from the government, which only came when in April 1940 Prime Minister Chamberlain was replaced by Churchill and Ernest Bevin, the former TGWU general secretary, became Minister of Labour.

Under Bevin collective bargaining across industries and services was given a push and in local government this meant that plans were soon being laid for a National Joint Council for County Roadmen. By the autumn of 1940 the new council had a constitution. It gave regional councils the power to determine wages, which NUPE believed was 'too permissive' but was prepared to accept; as the President, Bobby Whitlam, said to national conference in 1941, 'they felt confident that the infant would, with careful nurturing, outgrow that apparent weakness.'

In the perilous spring months of war in 1940, roadworkers were transferred to work on the land as food shortages became acute. Bevin had consulted NUPE about this and had received support from the union on the condition that the workers' conditions would be protected and it would only last for the period of the emergency.

The rapid rise in prices accompanying war conditions was immediately recognised by NUPE as a problem for low paid workers. Roberts, in a circular to organisers in October 1939, wrote that members were asking what the union was doing about the rising cost of living. 'If they are not reasonably satisfied that we are doing something we shall inevitably register membership losses.' At national level, Roberts was trying to convince the two general unions that a cost-of-living bonus should be established nationally, but they stuck by their belief in negotiation at provincial council level Roberts regarded this as, 'a first class blunder... the other unions are in my view blind to the realities of wage problems in the local government service.'

EXECUTIVE COUNCIL, 1945-47

Back Row : Bros. F. McFetters, F. Gould, Sister S. Kime, Bros. J. Cardwell, W. S. Wigg, T. I. Barnes, Sister F. Marriott, Bros. J. Roper, H. J. Knight
Front Row : Bros. A. Clark, S. Lawther, H. J. Catchpole, A. Tugby (*President 1945-46*), W. Stevens (*President 1946-47*), Bryn Roberts (*General Secretary*),
R. F. Jones, F. P. Hill (*Finance Officer*).

Executive Council 1945-47.

Back row (left to right) *Frank McFetters (Edinburgh), Frank Gould (Wallasey), S. Kime (Redhill), Jack Cardwell (Blackpool), Sam Wigg (Norwich), T. Barness (Pinewood), F. Marriott (Chislehurst), Jim Roper (Dudley), A.H. Knight (Ewell).*

Front row (left to right) *A. Clark (Exeter, Steve Lawther (Blaydon), Harry Catchpole (Ardsley), Arthur Tugby (Nottingham – President 1945-6), Bill Stevens (London – President 1946-7), Bryn Roberts, Richard Jones (Merthyr), Fred Hill (Finance Officer).*

NUPE was able to point to the wide variations that existed in the cost of living payments, from five shillings a week in Middlesex to two shillings in the South West, and when in April 1940 the Administrative, Technical and Clerical JIC agreed a national bonus, the argument had been won and it was only a matter of months before it was conceded at the Non-Trading JIC.

Relations with the general unions continued to be fragile, with allegations of 'poaching' consistently being made against NUPE – with Roberts the architect. In reply to a NUPE motion at the 1941 TUC calling for a more rational trade union structure Charles Dukes of General and Municipal Workers said: 'I venture to suggest to Bryn Roberts that when he begins to play cricket, we can have an arrangement with the union.' NUPE however, didn't want arrangements which hemmed the union in. It believed it was bringing into the ranks of organised labour workers who had been neglected by trade unions, and who no-one – not even the powerful general unions – had a monopoly over.

Roberts would not compromise NUPE's expansion for what he saw as a cosy relationship with its competitors. On at least one occasion he rejected personal offers of alternative employment that would have secured him a parliamentary seat and a place on the General Council of the TUC.

In return, the general unions continued their domination of the negotiating bodies, where the representation reflected not the current distribution of members but that of twenty years before. In 1945 NUPE had fifty-eight seats on the national and provincial councils, compared to the one hundred and twelve of the Transport and General Workers and one hundred and thirty-two of General and Municipal Workers, despite the fact that NUPE had more members in local government than the TGWU and probably as many as the NUGMW.

More blatantly unfair was the way the general unions had worked together to exclude NUPE from any of the official positions on the roadmen's negotiating bodies. Roberts wrote to Bevin about this in June 1941 protesting that although NUPE had clearly the majority of members, the two unions between them held every secretaryship and chairmanship across the country.

Roberts also sought the Ministry of Labour's support for NUPE's campaign to win back the seats on the Midlands JICs. Bevin refused to intervene but the union received a big boost when the employers' side of the South Midlands JIC backed NUPE's claim in October 1941. The NUPE Executive decided at this point to take drastic action and instructed its officers to present themselves at meetings where conditions of service of NUPE members were being discussed. The East Midlands JIC was chosen because it treated NUPE 'least considerately' and on 10 December 1941 three officers (Arthur Moyle, Sid Hill and H.G. Knight), and George Rastall of the Executive, sat in at the meeting. The secretary asked the NUPE delegation to leave, to which the national officer, Arthur Moyle, replied, later telling the press the content of his speech:

> I said with the greatest of respect to the position of the chairman and the Council I was unable to leave the room, because I had a higher duty to perform. We denied the right of the Council to exclude us from representation while they reached any decisions on policy affecting the status of our large membership in the area.

The meeting was held up for half an hour. The police were called and asked the delegation to leave, which they did.

The sit-in was not repeated again, as the Executive decided that it had achieved its objective of attracting publicity. A motion was then submitted to the 1942 TUC calling on the General Council to investigate the injustice against NUPE and this brought the matter to a head. During Congress, Roberts was approached by Arthur Deakin, general secretary of the TGWU and Charles Dukes, who agreed to NUPE having four seats on the East, West and South Midland JICs on condition that the motion was withdrawn. The NUPE delegation recognised a victory and agreed to withdraw the motion.

NUPE also enjoyed success in October 1941, when a Buckinghamshire County Council roadworker won a case in the High Court – with the union's backing – against the payment of wages by cheque. The decision sent county treasury departments into confusion and slowly they were forced to change their arrangements and pay their roadmen in cash. By June 1942 ten authorities had followed the court ruling. The Association of County Councils, however, made representations to the Home Secretary Herbert Morrison to reverse the decision. Bryn Roberts asked for permission to put the union's case before the Home Secretary but was refused, forcing him to issue an 'open letter' in which he declared that he hoped that Morrison would not become known as, 'the man who, in defiance of a High Court Judgement, fastened the cheque system with all its evils on the humble county roadworker.' Morrison ignored NUPE's plea and used his powers in 1942 to introduce a defence regulation permitting County Councils to pay roadmen by cheque. This regulation stayed in effect until December 1947.

If NUPE remained unhappy with this example of government interference in labour relations, it soon recognised the progressive nature of other measures, including the introduction of arbitration procedures, which were used on numerous occasions to force backward authorities to abide by JIC agreements. Bryn Roberts, in particular, understood that the central planning, direction and co-ordination functions undertaken by the Government in war could be the harbinger of a socialist future and for this trade unions needed to prepare by getting their own structures right.

PLANNING FOR POST-WAR RECONSTRUCTION

Speaking to a NUPE motion at the 1941 TUC on trade union re-organisation, Roberts set out this perspective:

> Private enterprise without state aid has demonstrated its inability to meet the needs of the present war... post war problems will involve national planning and a great programme of reconstruction which will effect extensive changes in the entire life of our nation. I believe it will also give the trade union movement the greatest opportunity it has ever had

to influence the character of these changes and to implement the principles of real industrial democracy. But is the trade union movement in proper shape to grasp these opportunities?

Roberts answered 'no' to this question because the trade unions organised along 'conflicting' lines giving rise to 'rivalries and competing activities.' Given this, Roberts argued that it was a contradiction for trade unions to:

> condemn the competitive principles of private enterprise and its planless and chaotic operations and at the same time shut our eyes to those very features which characterise our own movement … we want to plan industry, we want to replace capitalism, we want to reconstruct the bloodstained world. Let us start by attempting to plan and reconstruct ourselves.

NUPE's motion called on General Council to enquire into the structure of the trade union movement to decide whether general unions should be circumscribed or permitted to extend to all industries; whether existing boundaries of craft organisations should be altered and whether greater efficiency could be obtained through trade union organisation by industry. Not surprisingly the big guns from the general unions lined up to speak against the motion, among them Charles Dukes who said:

> I think we shall get greater unity. It may not be quite scientific, but very few things in this world are… The more we can progress along the lines of adaption the better for the spirit of the movement … I would suggest to Bryn Roberts that there is far more useful work for the trade union movement to do.

The motion received 2.5 million votes and was only defeated by 164,000 votes – a very close result considering the influence of general and craft unions at Congress. The war was unmistakably radicalising the trade union movement and NUPE's championing of a new perspective was winning support.

During 1942 Bryn Roberts visited America with a TUC delegation and his contact with the Congress of Industrial Organisations (CIO) confirmed his belief in the need for the British trade union movement to re-organise in anticipation of the war ending. This support for the CIO and insistence that the TUC act to establish international trade union co-operation played a major part in setting up the World Federation of Trade Unions in 1945.

NUPE can also claim some credit for its role in an important resolution passed at the 1943 TUC on post-war reconstruction. NUPE's original motion emphasised social ownership as the basis for British industry after the war, but if its content was slightly lost in the compositing process, Roberts was able to drive the message home when he spoke:

> The national crisis has compelled the application of many socialistic principles. These have, under actual test, even under the most unfavourable conditions, proved more effective and efficient than those of free enterprise. In the very heat and the turmoil of war our socialist faith has been vindicated.

The motion called on the General Council to prepare a plan for post-war Britain which reflected the central role played by trade unions in the life of the country and which recognised the need for full employment, public ownership and control of industry. The Economic Committee of the General Council set to work on preparing the plan, receiving submissions from unions, including NUPE, which naturally emphasised the importance of public ownership and trade union involvement in decision-making. The resulting interim report on post-war reconstruction was presented to the 1944 congress and became a central document informing Labour Party policy and the content of the 1945 election manifesto *Let us Face the Future*.

The Labour landslide victory of 1945 saw two of NUPE's most able organisers successful in winning seats in Parliament: Arthur Moyle was elected for Stourbridge, and London organiser, Arthur Bottomley, was returned for Chatham. Together they were to constitute the first direct NUPE representatives in Parliament, ensuring that the interests of union members were advanced – particularly as the Labour government set up a comprehensive welfare state in which NUPE

London dustmen in 1937.

members would be employed.

The Executive were aware of these developments and began reshaping the union so as to take full advantage. Sydney Hill, formerly divisional officer in the West Midlands, brought his considerable negotiating experience to head office, as he became national officer. The nationwide organisation was broken up into divisions, with divisional officers in charge of the area officers who were encouraged to specialise in the representation of members in either local government or health.

Bill Griffiths, a full-time trade union officer formerly with COHSE (the Confederation of Health Service Employees) was employed to help give direction to the organisation of the growing number of health workers in the National Health Service which was set up in July 1948.

THE INCREASING INVOLVEMENT OF WOMEN

Specialist attention was given to the women employed in the school meals service which had emerged during the early years of the

war and had been boosted by provision in the 1944 Education Act that local education authorities must provide a mid-day meal for children whose parents wanted them to have it. New branches of the union were established consisting entirely of school meals staff and they brought into NUPE a new enthusiasm, as Alan Fisher, then area officer in the West Midlands, wrote in 1948:

> Another remarkable feature is the way in which our new women members attend union meetings. At special meetings held in Oldbury, Smethwick, Tipton and Coventry... over 90 per cent of the entire school meals staff have been present.

Women began to play a more active part in the union in these years. The office of branch secretary – formerly a male bastion – began to be filled by women. Three women were elected to the Executive in 1943 (the first had been elected in 1939) and more women attended conference as delegates and made contributions to debate. At the 1949 conference the Doncaster delegate, Sis-

Although Roberts was on the left of the labour movement, he had little time for the Communist Party which he described in 1942 as

❛ a helpless collection of well-meaning people who have committed so many errors themselves that they are obliged to spend the greater part of time explaining them away. ❜

Communists were active within NUPE and at the 1943 National Conference they won support for a resolution backing the affiliation of the Communist Party to the Labour Party. Executive Council member H.J. Knight dismissed allegations that communists were trying to disrupt the labour movement and described how

❛ the building of his own branch was largely the work of communist members, all of whom paid the political levy, yet were debarred from representing the branch in the local Labour Party. In that situation it was not the communist member who was deprived of his rights; the whole branch was disenfranchised because none but communists could ever be found to take on the work. ❜

The policy was overturned at the 1945 NUPE National Conference but NUPE did not embark on an anti-communist campaign like a number of other unions in the late 1940s.

ter Curry, called for the appointment of women organisers, remarking that although more women were involved in the union, they were not represented by women full-timers. She cast her eye around the conference and expressed her disappointment at the 'disgraceful state of affairs' that the hall was full of men representing 170,000 members – half of whom were women. The Executive promised conference it would keep the situation under review and appoint women organisers when it thought appropriate.

The growing commitment of women to the union was rewarded in the post-war years by the establishment of national negotiations in services which were overwhelmingly female.

A severe shortage of labour in the hospital domestic service had forced the government to set up a committee, under Hector Hetherington, to investigate. Arthur Moyle, in 1943 still national officer, had no doubt about the problems.

I charge the hospital managers with the responsibility for the plight we are now in. For the shortage of staff in the hospital services is a pre-war problem, aggravated by war and it is the direct result of cumulative neglect of hospital managements over a period of years... in so far as domestic employment was

concerned (in the voluntary hospitals) they relied in the main on casual labour hired at rates of pay and conditions which were a disgrace to a civilised community.

NUPE advocated national determination of wages and conditions for hospital domestic staff – a remedy the Hetherington Committee broadly accepted. A Joint Council was established in 1945 to be superseded by the Ancillary Staff Council in July 1948, as the comprehensive Whitley machinery came into effect under the NHS.

A national agreement for school meals staff was also introduced in 1948 which gave significant improvements in wages and conditions for thousands of women – notably on paid holidays. Similar agreements were also negotiated across the public services, most significantly in the local government Non-Trading JIC, where in March 1947 it was decided that all wages would be determined nationally – based on one rate for London, another for towns and cities (zone A) and another for rural areas (zone B).

DIFFICULT TASKS

While NUPE was able to celebrate and claim considerable credit for these achievements, it was soon clear that the country's economic position was imposing severe restrictions on the negotiators. The war effort had placed a heavy burden on the economy, causing a large gap to open up in the balance of payments, which the government attempted to address by limiting the growth in incomes. At a special TUC conference in March 1948, Bryn Roberts expressed NUPE's backing for the TUC's policy of standing with the Labour government, but on the condition that it was a short-term measure designed to overcome the immediate problems. Roberts declared that NUPE could not give its support to a policy which pegged workers such as county roadmen on five pounds a week indefinitely, 'while the fashion parades at Ascot and Aintree and countless others were left untouched.' What was needed, Roberts argued, was a thorough-going socialist economic policy of expansion, planning and nationalisation. The TUC had a duty to propose these alternatives, because it represented millions of working-class people, whose living standards were at risk. And if the TUC didn't initiate proposals, Roberts would soon be at the speaker's rostrum, as he was at the 1949 Congress, criticising the TUC statement on the crisis which he believed to be a 'confession of helplessness':

> We are to mark time, that is what it amounts to. We are to hope for the best. If the General Council believes that the crisis should be solved by increased production, by greater exports, by more effective control over profits and prices, then let the General Council produce plans showing how these objectives can be reached.

Bryn Roberts firmly believed that the crisis facing the Labour government presented the trade union movement with a major challenge to pose radical solutions, which would begin to move society away from the anarchy of capitalism and towards the planning of socialism.

In an article in 1948 he linked these changes to those that had occurred in collective bargaining:

> just as local negotiations give place to regional negotiations and regional to national, so in turn the national negotiations in each industry must be subject to an over-riding central control, for in no other way can a planned economy on socialist lines be established.

The TUC did not respond with the required initiative and the Labour government began to lose direction. Roberts attributed these failings to the structure of a trade union movement organised not on a rational and planned basis, but on a chaotic and competitive format – dominated by powerful vested interests.

He passionately believed that organisation and planning, combined with flair and imagination, could transform any situation. In support of this formula, he could point to NUPE's achievements since 1934, when it had only 13,000 members and was in danger of being swallowed up by one of the general unions. By 1949 NUPE was itself a powerful force with 170,000 members whose voice could not be ignored. It had performed the herculean task of organising county roadworkers, which had helped build a trade union and political consciousness in rural areas – an important factor in the 1945 Labour victory. NUPE had led the agitation for a comprehensive system of national collective bargaining across the public services, which by 1948 was in place. And it was beginning to reach part-time women workers with the union message that they too deserved good wages and conditions.

These achievements – won against all the odds – helped give NUPE members a great pride in their union, which many regarded as an extension of their family. Members would give up annual holidays to go on recruiting exercises. County roadmen would cycle miles in the dark to attend meetings. Branch members would attend dinners, socials, excursions and rallies in the hundreds.

This loyalty grew out of NUPE's determination to change the way things were, to give a collective voice to the exploited and under-valued public service workers and demand fair treatment, to give a sense of personal worth to all workers – whether 'skilled' or 'unskilled', man or woman, full-time or part-time. These were the lasting achievements of NUPE's great expansion.

6. Towards a wider role

1949-62

Patients registering for health care under the new NHS at the London Hospital in April 1949.

TORY YEARS

The post-war move towards national wage setting did not prevent the pay of public service workers from continuing to lag behind the average in industry. A Ministry of Labour survey in 1950 found an average male industrial wage of seven pounds two shillings and eight pence compared to the local authority manual workers' basic of five pounds thirteen shillings and six pence. Rising prices further undermined wage levels in local government and the health service, where there were fewer opportunities for additional earnings through overtime and bonus payments. At the 1951 National Conference, Bryn Roberts told delegates that because of inflation their wages – in terms of what they would buy – had fallen back to the level of 1938 and that despite over five years of Labour rule: 'The social relationships and inequalities of 1951,

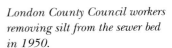

London County Council workers removing silt from the sewer bed in 1950.

HULTON DEUTCH COLLECTION

still bear too close a resemblance to the pre-war days'.

Occasionally members would, out of frustration, take industrial action, like the Edinburgh dustmen who went on unofficial strike in September 1951. Roberts didn't approve of the strike and he visited Edinburgh personally to persuade the men to return to work and await the union's negotiations.

The situation facing NUPE members dete-riorated following the election of a Conservative government in October 1951 who insisted on interfering in collective bargaining while at the same time cutting funding for public services.

The school meals budget was hit hard, forcing education authorities to cut the hours and wages of staff. The service was also undermined by successive price increases which hit demand dramatically, as in 1956

Come along Mary!

The union began to recruit nurses with some success in 1937. In 1938 the small National Association of Nurses joined NUPE. This leaflet dates from 1950.

when the numbers having school meals fell by nearly a quarter of a million following a two pence increase.

The health service was also subjected to Tory cuts, which in 1953 forced a reduction of 5% in staffing levels – a policy contrasted with increased military spending by Executive Council member Ivor Davies, at the National

Conference of that year: 'There is something radically wrong when £1,600,000,000 are being spent on armaments and only £400,000,000 on the Health Service.'

The health service in these Tory years proved to be a difficult area in which to make progress – chiefly because the Government was able to influence negotiations directly.

Indeed NUPE complained bitterly about government interference in the Whitley system, which was being undermined by the Minister's insistence that all significant claims go through his department. Claims were more often than not being sent to National Arbitration Tribunal after a failure to agree on the negotiating body.

The trade union claim for a reduction in the working week for ancillary staff in the NHS, from forty-nine to forty-four hours, dragged on without resolution. It appeared repeatedly at arbitration tribunals, each time the unions presenting extensive evidence of how the forty-four hour week had been conceded across a wide range of industries and services – including local government in 1947. This was rebutted by the employers argument that it could not be afforded. NUPE took the issue to the 1954 TUC, allowing Bryn Roberts to set out the problem to representatives from the wider trade union movement who, as he remarked, already enjoyed a 44 hour week. He went on,

> The 48 hour week (which nearly 200,000 ancillary employees now work) has already created a grave Labour problem. Large numbers of the best and most experienced employees are leaving constantly for other jobs. Tens of thousands of pounds are being spent on advertising for replacements, but those who apply for the vacant jobs only remain for a short time. Meanwhile the chaos grows and the efficiency of the service is being undermined.

The NUPE campaign for a forty-four hour week stepped up with mass protest meetings of members – a new development – in Leeds, Liverpool and Manchester. The London meeting in March 1956 brought together more than three thousand members, many women, forcing three separate meetings to be held in the Caxton Hall. The meeting listened to a powerful speech in support from Members of Parliament Will Griffiths, and Bryn Roberts, who made it clear that NUPE would be looking for activity to raise the issue publicly. But in response to calls for a strike he said:

> We shall resist them with all our vigour. We

Bryn Roberts in full flow at the 1952 Labour Party Conference Tribune rally.

POPPERFOTO

shall not take strike action. We shall not, in any way, injure the patients' welfare, but we shall by every conceivable means do our utmost to embarrass the Ministry and organise public opinion in support of our claim.

Much public campaigning was undertaken by the union in pursuit of this demand, eventually conceded in 1958, with the result that NUPE became more closely associated with the health service, aiding recruitment and organisation.

The antipathy to strike action expressed by Roberts in 1956 rested on his belief that, with compulsory arbitration in place, it was unnecessary. Claims could be assessed on their merits by independent adjudicators, 'instead

FOR MEMBERS ONLY

President 1947-8
W. S. WIGG

President 1948-9
H. J. CATCHPOLE

NATIONAL UNION OF PUBLIC EMPLOYEES

National Biennial Conference
HASTINGS
May 22nd, 23rd and 24th, 1949

SPECIAL REPORT

RE

CLAIM FOR FACILITIES TO ENABLE THE UNION TO MAKE REPRESENTATIONS TO THE CENTRAL ELECTRICITY AUTHORITY AND ITS AREA BOARDS ON BEHALF OF ITS MEMBERS EMPLOYED IN ELECTRICITY UNDERTAKINGS IN RESPECT OF THEIR TERMS AND CONDITIONS OF EMPLOYMENT AND OTHER LABOUR QUESTIONS

General Secretary
BRYN ROBERTS

Registered Office : CIVIC HOUSE BLACKHEATH, LONDON, S.E.3
Telephone : Lee Green, 2842-3-4-5

LEICESTER CO-OPERATIVE PRINTING SOCIETY LTD.

Despite disputes with the ETU, NUPE organised electricity workers in the public workers in the public sector from the 1920s. In 1947-8 they campaigned, unsuccessfully, for representation at the national negotiating body of the newly nationalised industry.

of uncontrolled capitalist might riding roughshod over the workers.'

Moreover, many NUPE members, Roberts wrote in 1951, would not engage in strike action: 'I cannot conceive the large army of hospital and health service workers resorting to strike action, or the many local government workers.' Arbitration gave such workers, dealing directly with the public, a power others had through their ability to upset production.

The TUC has since 1945 been pressured by a number of leading unions involved in

manufacturing to urge the government to remove the war-time order which guaranteed arbitration. NUPE resisted this, informing the TUC that it was the only instrument available to force backward authorities to abide by JIC decisions. Roberts also believed arbitration should remain as it was one of the building blocks of socialist planning, which the TUC needed to promote in a bold industrial policy. This industrial policy would have at its centre a long term wages policy which, he told the 1953 TUC, would allow for a more stable and equitable distribution throughout the movement. These views formed part of Roberts's much wider views about the future of Britain, based on socialist planning, industrial democracy and public ownership.

Roberts played a key role in the debates about the future of nationalisation in the labour movement in 1950s, associating himself very closely with the left Tribune group and successfully proposing an important motion at the 1952 Congress, calling on the General Council to formulate proposals for more ownership. The interim report presented to the next Congress did not please the NUPE delegation as it recommended the extension of public ownership to only the water industry. Roberts unsuccessfully moved a reference back of the report, commenting on the TUC General Council's speaker that, 'Mr Geddes stressed the desirability of filling the vacuum between capitalism and communism, but all this report proposes to do, is to fill it with water.'

Another Conservative victory in the 1955 general election didn't augur well for NUPE members who were accustomed to squeezes on wages and cut-backs in services. The annual round of national negotiations became an exercise in extracting from the employers small concessions, which did little but maintain the position of public service workers near the bottom of the pay league table. Some groups did make progress; caretakers and parks and gardens staff got national agreements in 1958 and 1959 respectively. And roadworkers benefitted from being included in the manual workers JIC, but across the union membership of 200,000 by 1957, discontent was growing, forcing even the General Secretary to reconsider his publicly stated attitude to varieties of union action.

During the 1950s, women members began to play a more prominent part in the union, and at the 1955 National Conference Sister Ross, from the LCC Meals Service Branch, proposed that a Women's National Conference should be held biennially. She said:

❝ there was an urgent need to give more attention to the special requirements of the women members. Women nowadays have two jobs to do – they have to work during the day and then come home to attend to household duties. Consequently, to be active in the union required a double effort from them; therefore, they required great encouragement if they were to play the greater part in union affairs which was essential... The first step was to let women speak for themselves and a National Conference of Women would be a start in that direction. ❞

Bryn Roberts replied to the motion on behalf of the Executive Council and asked the mover to refer it to the Executive, which was agreed.

His leading article in the Journal in January 1957 warned the employers of the growing feeling among members and their willingness to take action in defence of living standards, particularly as it was now clear that the Whitley Council and arbitration machinery had proved a failure:

If the real standards of our members continue to decline and the representatives of employing authorities remain indifferent to the wage claims properly submitted to them through the normal channels of negotiation and continue to depend on the trifling amounts which the Tribunals may award, NUPE could not counsel its members to grin and bear it.

Despite this threat, the next few years saw the gap between manual workers in the public services and others open as overtime and bonus payments became a larger percentage of the wage in the private sector. By 1960, the average wage in industry was fourteen pounds ten shillings and a penny compared to the basic nine pounds seven shillings and ten pence in local authorities. Discontent simmered among NUPE members, but it did not explode nor was it constructively articulated into action by the union.

Not that any of NUPE's competitor unions were any more inclined towards militant action. These were difficult years in the public services, as government insisted on restricting the growth in earnings severely because it was unable to have any real control over the activities of the private sector.

SHOP STEWARDS

Where NUPE did, perhaps, fail to seize an opportunity was in the early development of shop stewards. Stewards in many unions were beginning to take on a new role, as they ceased to be collectors, with union contributions deducted at source by the employer, and became local union representatives. NUPE did have stewards recognised by the employer in a number of areas, such as Southend and on the LCC estates building branches, but their functions were not clear and relationships with the union organisation undefined. An attempt to clarify the role of stewards was presented to the 1957 national conference by the Ramsgate Branch, who proposed a motion defining the role of the shop stewards as inspecting members' cards, reporting a change or violation of accepted conditions, and representing members, 'providing that no question involving a principle, change of practice or stoppage of work shall be determined by the shop steward'. The Ramsgate delegate drew an analogy between the union and a boy who had reached the stage when his clothes became too small for him: 'The time had come for the union to have a new suit. In short, they needed a new union structure in keeping with its developments.' The motion was referred to the Executive Council for consideration but the minutes are silent about further discussions.

The Birmingham school meals branch grew in the 1950s and undertook a wide range of social activities. Here they can be seen on a visit to the House of Commons in 1954 accompanied by NUPE MP Arthur Moyle (pointing) and to his left, the Area Officer for Birmingham, Alan Fisher.

It was certainly not reported on at the 1959 conference and the initiative to develop stewards was lost.

Bryn Roberts held conflicting views about this issue. In one publication he credited shop stewards with holding together the 'ricketty, disorderly and competitive trade union movement'. And in another he criticised the TUC general secretary, George Woodcock, for suggesting that some trade union power should be devolved to the workplace. Roberts believed this would be disastrous, as union competition would soon lead to anarchy. This ambiguity was probably the deciding factor in the failure to follow up the 1957 motion and, as no strong lobby existed for stewards, it was allowed to fall away.

Organisationally the Executive were preoccupied with the membership figures, which from 1957 had been disappointing.

In the late 1950s, NUPE argued publicly for a cut in arms spending, and in 1959 it adopted a policy of unilateral nuclear disarmament. At the 1958 TUC Roberts proposed that the General Council begin discussions with the Labour Party to consider a programme of drastic cuts in military spending:

❝ The arms bill is the greatest single inflationary factor. It is the chief contributor to high prices. It is largely responsible for the reduction of capital investment, the go-slow in hospital, school, house and highway building. The drastic cuts in the social services, the uncivilised herding, like animals, of mental patients in old, dilapidated hospitals, can also be in part attributed to the arms burden… in the prevailing industrial and distributive set-up there can be little improvement in real wage standards while the economy is bled on such a scale by the military machine. ❞

The high turn-over of staff across the public services, caused by low wages and poor conditions, made recruitment hard work and, with competition by other unions hotting up, prospects were not encouraging.

In the health service, relations with COHSE had never been good, with allegations of poaching by both sides resulting in numerous hearings before the TUC Disputes Committee. In one case an ambulance driver from Truro, Richard Andrew, had in 1951 left COHSE because of dissatisfaction and joined NUPE. The TUC Disputes Committee ruled that he should be returned to COHSE, a decision NUPE tried to implement. But Andrews refused, taking out a case in the High Court against NUPE! Andrews's case against NUPE was that, by expelling him, the union was acting against its own rules, as the only grounds on which an expulsion could occur was when a member had brought the union into disrepute. Andrew won the case in July 1955, forcing a rule change at the 1957 conference giving the Executive power to terminate any individual's membership if it was necessary to comply with a decision of the TUC Disputes Committee.

The irrationality of the competition which gave rise to such cases was appreciated on both sides, and certainly NUPE delegates at national conference made requests for amalgamation talks. Roberts replied that the Executive would meet COHSE at any time but although talks were held in May 1959 between Roberts and the COHSE general secretary, Jack Jepson, about possible working arrangements, nothing positive came from it.

Relations with the general unions levelled out in the 1950s, as NUPE became more widely recognised and it was understood that it was not going to go away. Informal working arrangements were established at local level and, although there were still skirmishes, members of all unions sat together at works and joint consultative committees. This mutual toleration broke down at national level, where a special hostility was reserved for Bryn Roberts whose repeated attempts to win a seat on the General Council of the TUC were blocked by the combined vote and influence of the TGWU and NUGMW.

This rankled with Roberts, who would have liked to participate at the highest level of the

The President, W.J. Davies, from Harrow, with Sydney Hill (left) and Bryn Roberts (right) at the 1953 TUC.

trade union movement, but he would not compromise his independence which he claimed was in the union's interest. He also throughout the 1950s thrived on the freedom to criticise the TUC from, so to speak, the outside. NUPE was excluded from the decision-making process and could therefore take a contrary view. Not that he had a very high opinion of the General Council, as he told a Tribune rally in 1953:

a great responsibility rests upon that small group of men within the TUC General Council, who now shape and direct its policy. Every office, every appointment within the movement is within their gift. They favour only those who are obedient to their will and offer no criticism, which perhaps explains why there are so many silent men on the General Council.

Roberts subsequently argued that these weak-

*The school meals service grew
rapidly during and after the
Second World War, providing
NUPE with a new organising
opportunity. The photograph
shows school meals being
served in 1952.*

HULTON DEUTCH COLLECTION

nesses, deriving from the structure of the
trade union movement, were responsible for
the third Labour general election defeat in a
row in 1959. The Labour Party, he wrote in a
controversial book, had deserted its fundamental belief in public ownership, a process
the trade unions failed to resist. Indeed the
trade unions encouraged the growth of anti-
nationalisation amongst the population by
persisting with competitive practices which
gave rise to strikes and disruption.

THE DEATH OF BRYN ROBERTS

Always one to speak his mind, Roberts would
also back up his rhetoric with a punishing
schedule of work which, by the mid-1950s,
was having an effect on his health. He missed
the 1956 TUC because of an illness and he
was told to slow down by the doctors. The Executive were aware of the need to bolster the
senior officer structure to aid the work at national level, and over the next few years officers were promoted within head office, including Sydney Hill, who became Chief National Officer, and Sid Barton, Arthur Butterworth and Alan Fisher, who all in turn became national negotiating officers. In the Finance Department Fred Hill, who joined the

staff in 1937, retired and was succeeded by
W.H (John) Bull in 1959.

Bryn Roberts suffered a stroke in the
spring of 1961 and was unable to attend the
national conference in May. Sydney Hill took
over many of his duties and was subsequently
made Assistant General Secretary by the Executive. Roberts did return to work but within a few months it was clear that his health
would not stand the pace he set himself, and
in July 1962, at the age of 65 years, the Executive agreed to his retirement. He was retained in a consultative capacity, but as his
health deteriorated, work became impossible
and in August 1964 he died. The Executive
agreed to a fitting memorial to his life by establishing a scholarship at Ruskin College,
Oxford. A packed memorial meeting was
also held in London at which tributes were
paid by Vic Feather, Assistant General Secretary of the TUC, Michael Foot MP and James
Griffiths MP, then secretary of state for
Wales.

Naturally Sydney Hill, who had become
General Secretary in July 1962, paid tribute
to Bryn Roberts recalling early organising
work with which he also had been involved
following his appointment in the West Mid-

lands area in January 1935. In these years Roberts energised a flagging union with a sense of commitment and direction, showing it was possible to reach groups of unorganised municipal workers. The organisation of county roadworkers must surely rank as one of the outstanding trade union achievements of the twentieth century. The establishment of national negotiations across the public services certainly owed something to the rationalisation of industrial relations during and immediately after the war years, but NUPE's contribution was critical in cajoling government and local authorities into action. The need for national wage-setting to transcend the anarchy of local authority pay determination was undeniably a Roberts creation, born soon after the expansion plan was set in motion and presented to the 1936 national conference.

All Roberts's life's experience, and theoretical training, pointed to the need for centralised decision-making. At the Central Labour College he learnt how socialist economic planning would overcome the contradictions of the capitalist market; as a trade union officer in the South Wales coalfield he fought for district-wide agreements to lift and unify the miners; and as NUPE's general secretary he led the union into national collective bargaining.

Roberts, and other left socialists within the labour movement, associated these centralising views with a vision of the socialist future in which rationality prevailed and decisions were made on what was good for society and not just the interests of private profit. Although never a communist – indeed he was sometimes hostile to the Communist Party – he believed the Soviet Union had achieved great things through the application of

PUBLIC EMPLOYEES JOURNAL

MARCH–APRIL, 1960

CIRCULATION 135,000

"WHAT'S ALL THIS £14 AVERAGE PAY, JOE?"
"IT'S WHAT YOU GET IF ALL WAGES ARE SHARED EQUALLY"
"WELL, I SEEM TO BE SHARING A HECK OF A LOT WITH SOMEBODY!"

(The Ministry of Labour reports that £14 a week mark for men's average pay has been passed. The average pay packets in October, 1959 were £14.1.3 per week.)

Low earnings in the public services compared to private industry led to severe shortages of staff.

In his book, *The Price of TUC Leadership*, published in 1961, Bryn Roberts controversially attributed Labour's third successive electoral defeat in 1959 to the failings of the trade union movement to project a positive image to the public. This, he argued, arose because of the structure of the trade union movement, which was no more than 'a collection of countless parts without any effective ties... The movement's leaders cannot see beyond their own garden walls. He argued that:

❝ By their acts of omission and commission they [the trade unions] discredited public ownership; they made nationalisation a dirty word; they lamentably failed to exercise any influence over industrial struggles except to sit back and wait for attrition to force a settlement of the struggles; and by abandoning the inherently peaceful purposes of the trade union movement in national and international affairs they caused many trade unionists and other members of the public to believe that world peace would be more secure in Tory hands than it would be in theirs.❞

At the memorial meeting to celebrate Bryn Roberts' life and work in 1964, Vic Feather, the Assistant General Secretary of the TUC said:

' Many of the things that Bryn spoke about at Congress years ago are accepted by the trade union movement today as though they have never been different. But other ideas that Bryn mooted twenty years ago and more are only now coming up as subjects for discussion throughout the movement… (His) approach was always a frontal attack, a trumpet blast, a march, and every banner flying. The impact of all this effervescence was often disturbing. It was not because he was misunderstood; Bryn spoke too clearly and trenchantly to be misunderstood. It was disturbing because he meant it to be. '

rational central planning and advocated a similar approach in Britain. His set-piece TUC speeches gave expression to these views as he insisted that the trade union movement should set the agenda for Labour's political movement, with the demand for public ownership as its kernel.

He also advocated a more interventionist and centralising role for the TUC, which he linked with the programme for reform along industrial lines. His persistence in forcing the issue onto the agenda was never dampened, even though he knew the general unions naturally opposed it, and the TUC establishment retained the view of its general secretary, Sir Vincent Tewson, who in 1956 said, 'The TUC was not the master but the servant of the unions.'

Most interesting perhaps was Roberts' championing, through periods of pay policy, of a radical approach to wages which stressed the need to give priority to poorly paid public service workers in any plan for incomes.

Roberts was beginning to grasp, somewhat heretically, and against the free collective bargaining view of the left, the need to plan incomes just as it would be necessary to plan everything else in a socialist policy for Britain. He saw value in the post-war Labour government's incomes policy, believing it could be the beginning of a rational approach to wages through which public servants would benefit. As the reality of this policy surfaced and it became clear that it was a form of wage restraint, he distanced NUPE from it. However, he remained committed to a rational method of wage fixing which gave to those without collective bargaining power a leverage, a view which was later to be embodied in NUPE's

support for a statutory minimum wage.

Roberts the centraliser and planner naturally applied these practices in the union with much success in welding together a national union amid opposition from employers and unions alike. Members came together at branch meetings, at area conferences and every two years at national conference to agree policy, but nobody had any doubts about who was the driving force for the policies. Throughout the period of his leadership, there was a very real sense that the union was being directed from the general secretary's office at Aberdeen Terrace. Occasionally a challenge would emerge, but the sheer weight of his personality and prestige would ensure that the head office view prevailed.

It was inevitable, perhaps, that only an individual with such clear vision and determination, and at times ruthlessness, could have dragged the union from near oblivion to the ninth biggest in the TUC with 215,000 members in 1962. This leadership could also at times be intolerant and opinionated, but it was never without a flourish of Welsh oratory and bombast which, even when they disagreed with him, endeared him to the NUPE members.

These members joined the union because of what it could do for them through its experienced band of negotiators at area and national level. Many undoubtedly joined NUPE because of the General Secretary, who, in age of increasingly professional trade union officers, could still inject fire and passion into the union's message. Together they developed a sense of solidarity and association with the union, and as time changed it was given a new form and expression.

7. A new dynamism 1962-69

SYDNEY HILL

Sydney Hill had been with NUPE for over twenty-seven years when he became General Secretary in 1962. He knew the union from top to bottom, having served at area, divisional and national officer level, establishing a reputation as a first class negotiator. He had moved to head office after the war, and had become Bryn Roberts's close working colleague, leading important national negotiations. He did not, however, in these years, develop a major public profile – this was left to the General Secretary, who was a past master at attracting publicity – but he had a good working relationship with trade union officials from other unions, who respected his abilities. When he was nominated, therefore, for the TUC General Council in 1963, there was no organised opposition to him – as there had been to Bryn Roberts – and he was duly elected, causing Albert Armstrong, the union President in that year to remark, 'We've arrived at last.'

If Sydney Hill did not possess the charisma and oratory of Bryn Roberts, he did have a more collective approach to leadership, which allowed senior officers to make a substantial contribution to the union's development. At head office, Alan Fisher, now Assistant General Secretary, took on an important role, for which he was well fitted, as a leading advocate for union policy at TUC and Labour Party conferences. The national officers, Sydney Barton and Arthur Butterworth, grew in reputation as the need to provide specialist negotiating services became apparent. And in the appointment of Bernard Dix as research and publicity officer in 1963, the union acquired an able and experienced journalist capable of injecting a sharpness and professionalism into its written material. He soon revamped the *Journal*, giving it a new format and approach which was both popular and political.

Sydney Hill, General Secretary 1962-67.

If there were differences between the style of leadership of Sydney Hill and that of his predecessor, there were also similarities, most notably in the role the union continued to play at the TUC. At the 1962 congress, Hill seconded a successful motion calling on the General Council to examine the structure of the trade union movement and assess how it could be changed to meet modern conditions. In the subsequent discussion NUPE submitted comprehensive evidence in support of its belief that the movement needed to be reformed along industrial lines. The evidence highlighted the growing involvement by unions in complex discussions with gov-

A NUPE petition signed by thousands of people from the Midlands and the North of England, protesting at the rejection of a pay claim for nurses, was presented to the Ministry of Health in July 1962. NUPE sponsored MP Arthur Bottomley lends a hand.

ernment, which necessitated the TUC commanding the maximum support of affiliated unions operating in clearly defined areas. Technological developments also compelled change, by breaking down distinctions in work, and presenting workers with the possibilities of benefiting from the new processes. In the public services the need for industrial unionism was overwhelming: a united approach would help to prevent governments from cutting public sector wages as a tool of economic management.

To begin this process, NUPE proposed that the five unions affiliated to the TUC who organised exclusively in the public services – COHSE, FBU (Fire Brigades Union), HVA (Health Visitors Association), LCC Staff Association, and NUPE – should open negotiations on a new unified organisation. This, it was hoped, would encourage the general unions to stop organising in local government and the NHS. NUPE was never optimistic about the outcome of these negotiations even though it had an ally in the TUC

General Secretary, George Woodcock. The report to Congress in 1964 refused to accept a general case for industrial unionism. In presenting the report Woodcock advised delegates that:

> I think we really must take it that from now on it is not going to be worthwhile, for any considerable time at any rate, to raise this issue of industrial unionism as a general panacea for the British trade union movement.

The report did, however, encourage individual unions to seek amalgamations, including NUPE and COHSE, which Sydney Hill and his colleagues regarded as some recognition of the case for industrial unionism in the public services.

NUPE had also raised the treatment of health service employees at the 1962 TUC, suggesting an independent enquiry into the functions of the Whitley Councils, which, Hill said, had failed the staff:

Instead of providing pay and conditions that should be the envy of less happy workers, they have produced nothing but grave staff shortages, with ever lengthening waiting lists, closed wards and empty beds.

Interference in negotiations by 'office boys from the Treasury and messengers for the Ministry of Health' was subverting the Whitley system. Hill could also point to the over one hundred cases referred to arbitration in the NHS since 1948 compared to only six in local government as evidence of a flawed negotiating system. NUPE was at the time in dispute with the employers over a government pay offer of $2^1\!/_2$ per cent which brought thousands of members into protest during the summer of 1962.

There was a feeling developing among workers in these years that the long period of Tory rule had, through chronic under-funding, brought decay to much of Britain's social and economic structure. This was very apparent in the health service, with capital expenditure running below pre-war levels, 10,000 empty beds through staff shortages and half a million on waiting lists. The general shabbiness of the health service was illustrated by the Government's proposals for the introduction of private contractors – under the direction of Minister Enoch Powell – for catering, cleaning and gardening services.

NUPE received the full backing of the TUC in 1963 for its campaign against contracting out which Sydney Hill said would inevitably lead to a situation in which 'private profit gradually takes priority and the needs of the community are relegated to a very poor second place.'

A growing awareness of deprivation also characterised this period, as surveys revealed millions living in poverty – nearly half of whom relied on earnings and not benefits. The problem of low pay became closely identified with much public service work – a government survey in 1960 uncovering the statistic that at least four out of ten local government workers were earning below ten

In the early 1960s, university ancillary and technical staff began to join NUPE in large numbers. The union established strong branches at a number of the newer universities – quickly winning improvements for members. Recognition was not readily conceded in the established universities, as Alan Fisher told TUC delegates in 1965:

❙ In the cloistered citadels of our oldest universities – Oxford and Cambridge – the battle for proper trade union recognition has still to be won. I have a vivid recollection of leading a union delegation to meet the Council at King's College. I half expected to find a body of elderly gentlemen with mutton-chop whiskers, adorned in ruffs and lace. I was, to say the least, somewhat taken aback when a number of them confided to us that they were avowed socialists. And three openly declared their membership of the Fabian Society! It does not say much for the stamina of our intellectual friends that we are today still without proper recognition at King's College – or any other Cambridge college for that matter. ❚

NUPE's delegation to the 1963 TUC.

Back row (left to right)
T. Chipperfield, area officer Harold Plant, Public Relations and Research Officer Bernard Dix, E. Cooke, R. Milton, W. Hirst, D. Wallace, Fred Lockley.

Front row (left to right)
J. Kitchen, Executive Council member Bob Pinchin, Assistant General Secretary Alan Fisher, President George Morgan, General Secretary Sydney Hall, Executive Council member George Chatt, and P. Edwards.

pounds a week when the average for industry was fourteen pounds and ten shillings.

NUPE naturally wanted an end to the years of Tory misrule, but it also believed it was necessary for the labour movement to construct its own wages policy, as Sydney Hill described in 1963:

> The kind of wages policy we have in mind is one that can emerge only from the trade union movement itself. It would be a policy designed to secure the greatest advance in living standards for workers and their families. And it would be pursued in such a fashion that those who are at the moment on the back marks of the pay race move forward at a faster rate. In other words, we want to see a trade union movement acting as a movement and not as a loose collection of individual parts.

THE LABOUR GOVERNMENT AND INCOMES POLICY

If there were echoes of Bryn Roberts in these views, they would also have been detected by experienced delegates at the 1964 TUC, when Assistant General Secretary Alan Fisher described the acid test of economic planning as the ability to ensure that public service workers' wages keep pace with others. Within weeks of Congress, a Labour government under Harold Wilson was elected – albeit on

a slim majority – and the opportunity of improving the lives of working people opened up. Two NUPE sponsored MPs were returned, Arthur Bottomley in Middlesborough East and Richard Marsh in Greenwich, and the union looked to the future with guarded optimism.

The Labour government immediately set in place the National Board for Prices and Incomes (NBPI) which was to administer its prices and incomes policy agreed with the TUC and the employers' organisation, the Confederation of British Industry. A norm for pay increases of 3 to 3½ per cent was set, with a provision that this could be exceeded in cases of low pay. NUPE's Executive supported this policy, but with an insistence that low pay would indeed be taken seriously. At the national conference in May 1965, the Executive presented a statement to the delegates which set out with some clarity and perspective NUPE's views:

> It is widely believed that the primary purpose of an incomes policy is to stabilise prices, profits and wages and other forms of income in relation to the overall growth of in national production. This concept, however, can be a dangerous over-simplification if it leads to an acceptance of the present division of national wealth. We are convinced that an incomes policy based on social and economic justice

must assist in breaking down the present class structure of society by redistributing the nation's wealth in favour of the working class. For members of NUPE such a policy involves consistent and deliberate measures designed to secure a substantial increase in the earnings of public employees in order to narrow the existing earnings differential between public employees and workers in manufacturing industries.

There were other radical voices among the trade unions urging the Labour government to put redistribution at the heart of its incomes policy, but it soon became defined as a method of wage restraint and by July 1966 a six month freeze on wages was imposed, to be followed by a further six months of 'severe restraint'.

NUPE's Executive issued a statement opposing the freeze which it declared would hit low paid workers hardest, leading the union to 'draw the inescapable conclusion from these measures that the government has jettisoned the principle of social justice which is fundamental to the development of an effective prices and incomes policy': instead of freezing wages, NUPE advocated radical policies which recognised that Britain's role in the world had diminished and should be reflected in the value of the currency and the level of military spending.

NUPE took its views to the TUC in September 1966 with Alan Fisher making an outstanding contribution to a debate opposing the General Council's endorsement of the freeze. He told delegates how a quarter of a million local government workers, whose earnings were ninety shillings below the national average, would have received an increase of eleven shillings in the next few days but, 'It won't be there, it is as frozen as fish fingers.' What the General Council and the government should have done, 'if they wanted the full support of the unions, was to build a minimum wage into their policy so we all know what is really meant when we talk about low paid workers.' Although not successful in rejecting the pay freeze, NUPE – and a number of other unions – had stated the case that low pay should be taken seriously, forcing the TUC to reconsider its position, and over time it became more responsive to the issue.

the CHALLENGE of new unionism

the case for industrial unionism as a dynamic solution to the problems facing trade unionists

with an Introduction by
SYDNEY HILL
GENERAL SECRETARY
NATIONAL UNION OF PUBLIC EMPLOYEES

NUPE
pamphlet

6d

NUPE itself was becoming more aware of the inequalities built into the structures of low pay between men and women. The women's rate was only three quarters of the men's, a differential the union raised in a motion to the 1963 TUC calling for legislation to guarantee equal pay for equal work.

Women were becoming the majority of the union's membership in the 1960s and this was reflected at national conference, both in the subjects tabled for debate and the participants. One well-known delegate, Esther Brookstone, from the London (West) APTC branch, at the 1963 national conference pro-

A pamphlet written by Bernard Dix based on NUPE's evidence to the TUC enquiry into trade union structure following a motion at the 1962 Congress seconded by Sydney Hall.

London hospital workers began to take action to improve conditions in the summer of 1966. Ancillary workers at St. Andrew's Hospital, Bow, walked out in protest at excessive workloads caused by staffing shortages. NUPE members at Guy's and St. Mary's also took action in support of a claim for increased London weighting. The protest culminated in a large demonstration outside the Ministry of Health.

posed that the composition of NUPE's membership should be recognised in the union structure by creating two women's seats on the Executive Council. The Executive opposed the move on the grounds that all members of the union – men and women – had an equal right to put themselves forward for office. Although the motion was defeated, it had raised – perhaps ahead of its time – an issue that was to re-emerge with greater resonance in the next decade.

Part-time women workers were at the forefront of an important development in London in July 1966, when ancillary staff in a number of hospitals took industrial action in support of a claim for an increased London weighting payment. There were stoppages of work and picketing at hospital gates, culminating in a demonstration at the Ministry of Health's headquarters, which attracted a good deal of publicity. The *Journal* reported the enthusiasm of the demonstrators, who sent up a loud cheer, 'as hundreds of NUPE leaflets showered down on the Ministry building from the topmost part of a scaffolding on an adjacent construction site.' The ministry agreed to the union's request that the claim be referred to the NBPI.

FLEXIBLE POLICIES

The NBPI began a study of local government and Health Service wages and conditions in the autumn of 1966, immediately uncovering endemic low pay. Nearly one in four local authority workers earned less than thirteen pounds a week and nearly half earned less than fifteen pounds. In the health service the situation was slightly better, because of payments for shift and weekend working, but still one in five staff earned less than thirteen pounds a week compared to the national average of 6 per cent.

Aware that its efforts to increase the low basic rates through an incomes policy had not been successful, NUPE was encouraged by the NBPI study because it held out the prospect of increased earnings. The report, published in March 1967, gave a lack of 'earnings opportunities' as one of the key reasons for low pay in the local government and health services. This arose out of low productivity and inefficient use of labour, the result of poor management. As remedies the

A scene from the 1967 national conference.

report suggested improved management standards, better supervision, and most importantly, the application of local work-study schemes to increase productivity and earnings. In the short term the report suggested a series of interim payments to lift basic earnings of ancillary workers and roadmen by eleven shillings and eight pence.

Happy with these recommendations, NUPE trained local representatives in work-study and instructed them to push management to introduce productivity schemes, often coming up against great resistance.

Progress was slow and by 1969 only 10 per cent of local government employees were covered by such schemes, despite the evidence that earnings and productivity could be increased while costs were reduced.

The Executive was aware that there would need to be an increase in the number of union stewards to cope with the growth of local bargaining, and every encouragement was given to this, particularly in the provision

The Executive Council meet at the 1967 national conference.

of training. The decision of the manual workers' national JIC in January 1969 to recognise and provide facilities for union stewards gave an added impetus to the process and very soon the growing number of stewards were playing an important part in the union.

The willingness of NUPE to respond to these developments, with reforms in organisation, illustrated the way the union had changed – and was changing – from the previous era when the structure was set in space. At his final national conference in 1967 before retiring, Sydney Hill introduced a reform giving a bigger say to the membership, through national committees for local government, health and water, which were to be elected by branches and responsible for monitoring negotiations.

The delegates paid tribute to Sydney Hill for more than thirty years commitment to NUPE. In his reply to conference he said,

It has been a hard life, but an interesting one. I am happy in the knowledge that I came into the union when it was a struggling organisation, in fact it was often referred to as a 'pudding club'. I am pleased to know that when I leave it at the end of the year, it will be one of the most powerful – in terms of membership and prestige – of any trade union in the country.

Like his predecessor, Sydney Hill was retained by the union in an advisory capacity for twelve months after his retirement, a commitment he was unable to fulfil as he died in August 1968 at the age of 65 years.

THE ELECTION OF ALAN FISHER

Alan Fisher naturally was elected by the Ex-

NUPE has always been a very political trade union and during the 1960s its influence inside the Labour Party grew. A sharp political perspective developed, particularly around the debate on incomes policy. Much of this can be attributed to Bernard Dix, the Publicity and Research Officer, who with a grounding in left politics helped deepen NUPE's radical reputation. Typical of his contributions is this excerpt from a Journal editorial of October 1966, soon after the Labour government had imposed a wage freeze:

❛ Influential Labour politicians are claiming that the pay freeze, with Fabian-like stealth, is the first step to socialism. And they have already written off free collective bargaining as the first victim of the pale pink anaemia which now passes for red blooded radicalism.

Few trade unionists would claim that a free-for-all is an effective method of distributing the nation's wealth. It was never meant to be. It was merely a reflection of the free-for-all society in which the unions grew up and which – the Labour government notwithstanding – still exists.

When there is real evidence that this free-for-all society has a one way ticket out, the old-fashioned methods of wage-fixing will be easy to replace. And millions of trade unionists will be only too glad to see them go...

In most of the economy the old law of the jungle – no matter how cleverly camouflaged – still exists. If the government wants trade unionists to trim their toe nails it must first clip the claws of the tiger.❜

pay and productivity in local government
A BIG ROLE FOR UNION STEWARDS

ecutive in March 1967 to become General Secretary, having served as Assistant for five years. Before coming to head office, he had been area and divisional officer in the West Midlands, having started work for NUPE in 1939 as a clerk in the newly opened Birmingham office, alongside Sydney Hill. As national officer, Alan Fisher established himself as an effective negotiator – as secretary of the staff side on the Ancillary Staffs Council – and as a public speaker, with a number of impressive performances at the TUC. His considerable experience did not hold back new thinking and he was always open to ideas from any quarter, but most notably from Bernard Dix, who was emerging as a key figure in the policy making process.

Meanwhile the TUC was attempting to put together a policy on wages in response to growing hostility to the government's insistence on extending its powers over incomes, following the periods of freeze and severe restraint. At the 1967 Conference of Executives in February, NUPE supported a proposal for the movement itself to develop an incomes policy with its own priorities, one of which would be the need for low paid workers to receive bigger increases than others. Alan Fisher told delegates that his union backed this approach because, 'NUPE has enough confidence in the trade union movement and the working class to believe that we manage our affairs a lot better than any cabinet minister or civil servant.'

The positive role the TUC was developing was welcomed by NUPE who believed that it could help provide much-needed direction to the Labour government which had lost its sense of purpose. In a motion to the 1968 congress, NUPE called on the TUC to ex-tend its strategic planning in relation to the economy, social ownership, industrial democracy and education, with Bernard Dix declaring that, 'Now more than any time in its history, the TUC is the pivot around which the whole labour movement revolves.'

Relations between the trade unions and the Labour government were at rock bottom, and NUPE, in common with other TUC unions, opposed Employment Secretary Barbara Castle's plans for industrial relations reform, with penal sanctions for unofficial strikes. She was listened to in a strong silence when speaking at the 1969 NUPE national conference, and President Alf Uren summed up the mood of the conference when he made a reply to the minister:

> By rushing through legislation which is mainly concerned with punishing strikers, the government is missing a real chance to regain the confidence of trade unionists by co-operating with them and securing real and lasting improvements in industrial relations.

He went onto remark that, 'as a union we are not often involved in disputes of the kind that make newspaper headlines' – unaware, of course, that within months the discontent of workers would ignite into industrial action on the streets of London.

Feelings were running high among London's local authority workers in the summer of 1969 as negotiations in pursuit of a fifteen shilling claim ran into difficulties as the employers delayed. News of this spread to groups of well organised dustmen who decided to take action without union backing. Hackney dustmen stopped work in September, demanding an increase of five pounds

The introduction of work-study based productivity schemes in the late 1960s provided an impetus to the development of a steward system announced here in the union Journal of March 1969.

London dustmen on strike in October 1969.
POPPERFOTO

and sent out workers around the boroughs to win support. Within ten days nearly all the dustmen across the capital were out on strike and they were being joined by highway gangs, sweepers and park staff.

With rubbish piling up and the union fully behind the strikers, the employers faced the prospect of an official dispute that could spread. In a settlement which, the union *Journal* remarked, 'makes all previous rises look as old fashioned as a ha'penny piece,' increases ranging from fifteen shillings to two pounds were conceded, with improvements in London weighting, overtime and women's pay.

The lessons of the strike were not lost on the union as it assessed the significance of the victory. Confidence of the members was now sky high as they realised they could take on the employers and win. Negotiators would be able to press ahead with productivity deals in the knowledge that if employers dragged

their feet, members would act. And the union would step up its plan to establish an effective system of union stewards which Bernard Dix, writing in the union *Journal* of December 1969 saw as crucial:

> In this way NUPE can achieve the real partnership of modern militant trade unionism, with local and national negotiators playing their respective roles, supporting each other's efforts and winning real benefits for all local authority workers.

The strength of feeling and willingness of London members to strike surprised the union at first, but it was quick to respond, channelling the action towards the bargaining arena. The union travelled a long way in the three weeks of this dispute and it was sure that things had changed for ever. NUPE would enter the new decade confident and optimistic that it was moving forward.

8. NUPE in the limelight

1970s

For NUPE, the years between 1970 and 1979 were eventful, even tumultuous. Before the 1970s, the name of NUPE was scarcely known outside of its own members and professional trade union circles. Even amongst those who knew and understood British trade unionism intimately, NUPE hardly counted as one of the key players. The experience of the 1970s changed all that: by the end of the decade, the name and exploits of the public employees' union had been publicised in every medium of popular communication in the land, and by no means always accurately. Even so, in less than ten years, NUPE had moved from being one of the 'extras' to being centre stage in the public drama of British industrial relations.

GROWTH

What explains this rapid change of circumstances? Was it the mere fact that the union more than doubled in size in the ten years up to 1979, peaking at more than 726,000 members? Admittedly, this was a remarkable achievement and was accomplished, it should be remembered, not by amalgamation or by the acquisition of a series of ready-made but smaller partners, as some other noteworthy trade unions' growth had been achieved. NUPE's expansion in this period was, quite simply, the outcome of employment growth, improved organisation, recruitment, a general upward movement in union membership in the country and the early use of public service employers' preparedness to deduct union subscriptions directly from workers' wages.

However, growth was nothing new to NUPE. As we have already seen, once the union got over its membership crisis and the threat of its demise in the mid 1930s, continued membership growth became a constant feature of life in NUPE. From the time of Roberts's brilliant Expansion Plan onwards, recruitment and organisation had been the

Alan Fisher speaking in 1969.

watchwords of branch officials and full-time officers alike. In the late 1960s and 1970s, all candidates interviewed for appointment to the union's rapidly expanding force of full-time officials were closely questioned on their previous record of recruiting new members. Each month, members of one of the Executive Council's main committees examined a selection of activity reports from officers,

partly to review their organising and recruitment successes.

Amongst full-time officers of the union, it became something of a standing joke in the 1970s that the General Secretary, Alan Fisher (or 'the old man', as he was affectionately known), at their annual meeting with the Executive Council in Ruskin College, would invariably exhort them to re-double their efforts to recruit more members. Fisher's own employment with the union included an enviable record of successful membership recruitment in the West Midlands and he never failed to underscore its importance for NUPE's strength.

The General Secretary's other recurring topic at the Ruskin conference was the need for greater prudence in the use of the union's fleet of cars. These had been made available to full-time officers in order to facilitate their easier access to NUPE's widespread members and potential members, who typically worked in small, dispersed workgroups. This was quite different from the situation facing union organisers in factories, railways, docks and the country's then still numerous coal mines.

Thus, in membership terms alone, the years of the 1970s represented a sharp upward change of gear. NUPE not only exploited and benefited from the large expansion of jobs in local government and the health

service: its recruitment more than kept pace with employment growth and the proportion of the workforce organised into public service trade unionism also grew. By the end of the decade, no less than 78 per cent of local government and education workers and 74 per cent of health service workers were in trade union membership.

UNION GROWTH IN BRITAIN

In some ways, NUPE's rapid growth in the 1970s mirrored the growth of British trade unionism generally at the time, especially in the public services. To that extent, the explanation for NUPE's outstanding success in organising a further 300,000 members in less than ten years has to be set in the wider context of British trade union organisation of that period. It reached a peak of almost thirteen and a half million members (almost six out of every ten workers) by the time the first Thatcher government was elected in 1979. In less than a decade, the membership of British trade unionism generally had grown by one-third; in the same period NUPE's membership growth, which reached the level of 90 per cent, was three times greater.

Since that time, of course, British trade unionism has seen the loss of over 4 million members and NUPE itself has suffered a decline of almost 170,000. Just as NUPE's growth in the 1970s had been far greater than the average, so its losses in the much more difficult 1980s and 1990s, under successive attacks from four Conservative governments, have been far smaller than the average across British unions as a whole. This, in itself, is a praiseworthy achievement.

NUPE'S OBSCURITY

Even before its spectacular growth in this short period, NUPE was hardly a small trade union. On the contrary, by British standards at least, the union was already very large. By the time of the 1969 dispute and the failure of Harold Wilson's government to get itself re-elected in 1970, the union already organised 370,000 members and was the seventh largest union affiliated to the TUC. Yet, up to that time, the union's fortunes had scarcely ever figured either in public debate, or in scholarly discourse, or in the media representation of industrial relations. Nor did it seem to matter that, in the figure of Bryn Roberts, the union had possessed one of British trade unionism's most colourful, eloquent and publicity-conscious General Secretaries.

Roberts had served at the top of the union for almost thirty years, and had shouted its virtues and its yearned-for goal of industrial unionism in the public services from every labour movement platform he could reach. Less flamboyantly, but no less effectively, thousands of NUPE branch secretaries and full-time officials had toiled away daily at representing the union's members and righting their wrongs. Tens of thousands of workers in the public services had joined the union, eventually making it one of Britain's biggest. But still the union seemed not to merit extensive coverage or to excite serious study before the momentous years of the 1970s.

What explains this? The answer is three-

The Tory government's Industrial Relations Bill brough 140,000 trade unionists onto the streets in Spring 1971.

fold and lies, first, in the dominant character of British trade unionism up to that time. Secondly, it reflects clearly the employment circumstances of NUPE's members and, thirdly, it is a matter of the sheer visibility of trade union activity.

In the period up to the 1970s British trade unionism still bore clearly the distinguishing marks of its modern origins amongst manufacturing, miners and men. These were also the predominant concerns of those politicians, journalists and academics who pro-

The willingness of women member to take action in defence of the services they provided became a feature of the 1970s. This group of home helps from the West Riding of Yorkshire lobby County Councillors in Wakefield in April 1972 as part of a union campaign to improve the home help service in the area.

Health service workers across the country demonstrated in support of a pay claim in December 1972. In Nottingham a new meaning is given to the acronym NUPE, while in London Alan Fisher (in white mack) leads a march to the Department of Health and Social Security offices.

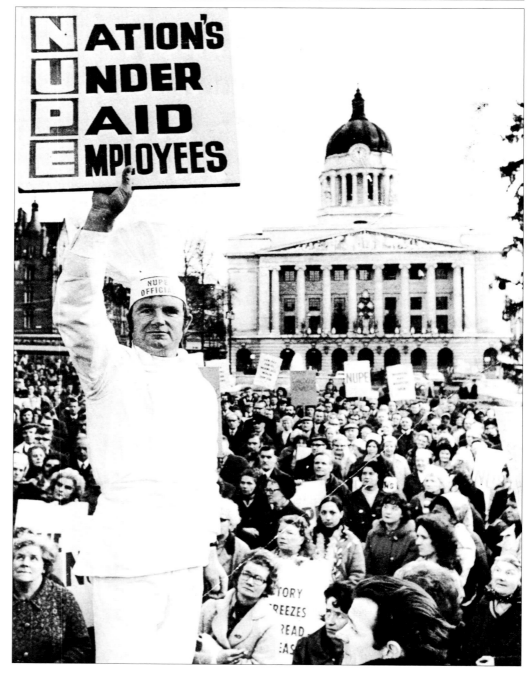

❝ Local authorities' services and the National Health Service contain large concentrations of workers whose earnings are among the lowest in the country...

The wage rate structures of the two services are so compressed that to increase the wage rates of the bottom grades, to an extent which would provide meaningful assistance to the lowest paid, would swamp many differentials in the structure and diminish others to the point at which they would lose significance. Such a course would inevitably result in pressures to restore the differentials. We are therefore compelled to reach the conclusion, given their present wage structures and limited earnings opportunities, that scope for wage increases confined to, or weighted in favour of, the lowest paid does not exist in the two services.

The corollary is that assistance to the low paid can be given only through a general increase in wage rates. But, if all workers in either industry were paid substantially more for the work now performed by the methods now in use, this would impose an unreasonable burden on the ratepayer and taxpayer and be incompatible with the requirements of prices and incomes policy. Therefore, any solution along these lines must be ruled out.

There is therefore no immediate answer to the problem of low pay in these services.❞

NBPI Report 29, *The Pay and Conditions of Manual Workers in Local Authorities, the NHS, Gas and Water Supply*, March 1967

nounced on trade unionism and the British industrial relations scene. Thus, the 'typical' trade unionist was taken to be a male in full-time paid work, representing workers in factories, docks, shipyards or mines. British unions were themselves characterised by institutions, practices, images and a language that owed little or nothing to manual workers and others providing services to the public in local authorities, the health service, in the water industry or higher education. Even though many trade unions outside the public services organised women workers, their voices were scarcely ever heard and their concerns rarely articulated.

For decades, workers in the public services had suffered exploitation by, and even the contempt of, employers whose own positions were underpinned by a potent mixture of their class, positions in the hierarchy, formal educational qualifications, professionalism and power. In some local authorities, councillors' dismissive attitude to a union composed largely of manual workers, such as NUPE, included an arrogance and self-deluding pomposity legitimated, in their own eyes, by their having been elected to office. In their opinion, the duty of public service workers was simply to serve and, hence, to be treated exactly as servants. Even the somewhat patronising notion of the 'dignity of the working man' was denied such workers.

Nurses from the Prince of Wales Hospital at Tottenham visit Downing Street as representatives of the staff side of the Nurses and Midwives Whitley Council meet Prime Minister Harold Wilson, in the summer of 1974. They presented the Prime Minister with a pipe which was accompanied by the works: 'We hope that you will consider it a pipe of peace, which it can be if you agree to give us more pay.'

In large part, of course, the trade unionism of these self-same public service workers was largely hidden from the public gaze and, thus, apparently also from their interest. Attention focused rather upon the often spectacular and much publicised confrontations between representatives of capital, labour and the state in shipbuilding, coal mining, the railways and docks, in engineering generally and in the motor industry in particular. Alongside these dominant centres of industrial disputation, an interest in NUPE's activ-

ities was limited to those directly involved and a few academic observers.

THE CHALLENGE BEGINS

The activities of NUPE in the 1970s were to institute a challenge to this partial and already somewhat dated picture of trade unionism in Britain. It is a struggle which continues today. By the end of the 1970s, NUPE's shift to the centre of the industrial relations stage had been marked, not only by the union's spectacular growth, but also by an unprecedented series of disputes and campaigns in the public services. These concerned pay (especially low pay), cuts in public expenditure, opposition to private practice in the national health service and arguments for alternative economic strategies to those pursued, successively, by the Conservative government of Edward Heath from 1970 to 1974 and the Labour governments of Wilson and Callaghan up to 1979. The decade culminated, of course, in the now infamous 'winter of discontent' of 1978-9, whose distorted image has been used ever since as a scourge, not only for NUPE, but for British trade unionism in general.

NUPE's case in the 1970s was powerfully

Above: In opposition to the Labour government's public expenditure cuts, NUPE rallied an impressive alliance of forces which took to the streets in protest in November 1976. Instead of cutting spending and so creating more unemployment, NUPE wanted the Labour government to change course and pursue socialist economic policies.
Below: Alan Fisher addresses the rally.

PAT MANTLE

articulated in the oratory of its energetic General Secretary, Alan Fisher. His two chief themes, of advocacy on behalf of disgracefully low paid workers, and of passionate defence of the public services, were soon familiar at the TUC and in the Labour Party. Increasingly, they were to be expressed with no less force before NUPE's own members, not simply in branch meetings and at union conferences, but also in public rallies and in the course of often bitter disputes.

A DECADE OF ACTION

NUPE speakers frequently found themselves alongside the leaders of other public service unions which were drawn, like NUPE, for the first time into large scale industrial and protest action. Postal workers, civil servants, teachers, hospital doctors, social workers and firefighters were all, at one time or another in the 1970s, engaged in strikes and other forms of industrial action, as were NUPE's members in local authorities, amongst ambulance staffs, hospital ancillary workers and nurses and even in the private and voluntary

sectors. With large scale strikes in the mines, and action in gas and electricity supply, disputes in the public sector accounted for almost half of all working days lost in the 1970s.

As it began to move from the shadows into the spotlight, neither NUPE nor the other public service unions were popular with governments, whose own policies were most frequently the first cause of the unions' actions. Nor, as we shall see, was NUPE's role in these disputes always popular with other unions or their leaders.

THE FIRST NATIONAL 'DIRTY JOBS' DISPUTE

NUPE's own leaders had been somewhat taken aback by the 1969 dispute and were determined that there should be no repetition the following year. As was to be the case so often in the next twenty years, government policy, or rather its limitations and perceived unfairness, was at the heart of the matter. When the Labour governments of 1964-70 had announced their national prices and incomes policy, they had always claimed that

As part of the campaign to win a sixty pound minimum wage across the public services, members took industrial action and demonstrated throughout the country. A national demonstration in London in January 1979 was attended by over 80,000 supporters. The Bermondsey banner, unfurled in 1937, is proudly displayed and provides a link with the union pioneers of the 1890s.

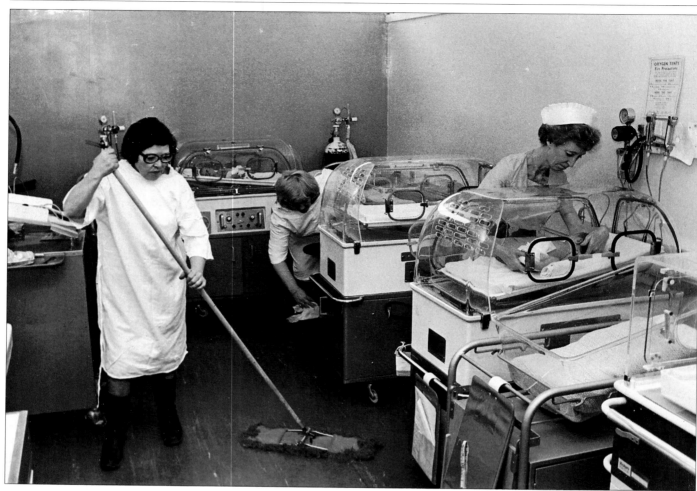

Throughout the dispute the union guaranteed members would provide cover in emergency services. At Harold Wood Hospital in Essex in February 1979 NUPE members take their turn on picket duty after working their shift in the special baby care unit.
POPPERFOTO

dealing with low pay would be a key part of their approach. Early on in the life of the National Board for Prices and Incomes, a report on the pay and conditions of manual workers in local authorities, the health service, and gas and water supply had acknowledged the problems of low pay in those industries, arguing that the key to its resolution lay in improved productivity and the application of incentive bonus schemes. Although such schemes began gradually to be introduced, especially for male manual workers in local government, their application was always partial and fragmentary. In any case, they did little to tackle the underlying causes and persistence of low pay.

Once more, towards the end of its period of office, the Labour government and the National Board for Prices and Incomes addressed themselves to the issue of low pay, and early in 1970 further studies were conducted resulting in further reports on the pay and conditions of manual workers in local authorities, ancillary workers in the NHS hospitals and on the general problems of low pay. But, by the time the reports had been

published, the Labour government had been defeated and Edward Heath's Conservative government had come to power with its face set firmly against the continuation of an incomes policy, whether statutory or otherwise.

By November 1970, the Heath government had announced the abolition of the National Board for Prices and Incomes, declaring instead that the settlement of pay was a matter principally between employers and representatives of employees. In any case, despite its several publications on the question of low pay, the Board's demise was scarcely to be mourned by NUPE. As the historian of the NBPI succinctly put it, the Board had accorded a lower priority to low pay than to other pay problems. Moreover, it did not see its role as arguing for any substantial shift in the distribution of income in society or for markedly disturbing established differentials.

Despite the Conservative government's opposition to Labour's incomes policy, Heath's approach, once elected, was systematically to set about lowering the value of wage settlements and therefore, it argued, lowering inflation. This resulted eventually in the so-

called 'N-1%' formula, intended progressively to reduce the level of wage settlements. Public sector pay settlements offered an ideal opportunity for such restraint. So began a decade of confrontation between public sector workers of all kinds and successive governments. For the first time, NUPE was in the thick of things.

Already in April 1970, before the fall of the Labour government, NUPE, the TGWU and GMWU had submitted a joint pay claim on behalf of more than three quarters of a million council workers. They were demanding a pay increase of two pounds and fifteen shillings, together with additional annual holidays and some improvements in shift pay. The employers' response was one pound and fourteen shillings.

When the New Earnings Survey was published for 1970, it showed that, in manufacturing industries, only 15 per cent of male manual workers and 78 per cent of female manual workers were earning less than eight shillings an hour. The comparable position in local government was 25 per cent for male manual workers and 90 per cent for women.

Whereas average gross weekly earnings for manual workers in all industries and services in April 1970 stood at almost twenty-seven pounds, the comparative figure in local government was twenty-one pounds. Full-time manual women's pay, which in any case was on average less than two-thirds of their male manual colleagues' earnings, stood at just over thirteen pounds weekly in the economy as a whole and the rate was very similar in local government.

Speaking at the TUC in early September 1970, Alan Fisher declared that NUPE found itself in 'a battle of vital concern' to every union representative in the TUC. He said,

We are not only involved in the first confrontation between public services and the government, but also involved in the first frontal attack on low pay. Pressure exercised by government on public services is not new, of course, our inferior pay position today bears testimony to this.

What is new is that for the first time ever, the General Council has said exactly what it expects the union to achieve in confrontation

> ❝ Let us make our position quite clear. We are absolutely committed to the belief that low pay is a scandal which can be, and must be, eradicated. We believe that low pay continues to exist in Britain because those who are, and who have been, in a position to do something about it have for too long been constipated by economic and political orthodoxy which - insofar as it is even prepared to admit that a problem of low pay exists - consistently argues that nothing practical or substantial can be done to remove it; an argument which is often used to cloak a conviction that nothing *should* be done to remove it. If we are to force a positive change in this attitude we need political action, which in turn rests on the need to promote organized, informed and articulate action by those who have the potential power to insist that a political solution is applied to the problem of low pay. Those who have this potential are primarily active trade unionists and their allies in the Labour Movement and the axe we are grinding must be used by them. ❞
>
> *Low Pay and How to End It*, Alan Fisher and Bernard Dix

to help out low pay. In pursuing this objective, my union finds itself poised on the brink of industrial action in a number of services for the first time during the 80 years of its existence...

We have reached the end of the line. Our members now say if the community will not pay the essential price for these services, then it has no right to expect them. Let me make it quite clear, as far as my union is concerned - and I say this in all seriousness - that if there is to be a fight, we are not going to chicken out.

Early in September 1970, the three unions rejected an improved offer from the employers of almost 14 per cent. Officials from the Department of Employment indicated that they would not be able to use their good offices to assist the unions to seek a settlement at a higher level. This response was not helpful to the unions and, at the end of September, a rolling programme of strike activity began in London and soon spread to other towns and cities across England, Wales and Scotland.

The strike ran from 29 September in England and Wales and from late October in Scotland, and was ended in the second week in November. Altogether about 125,000 workers became directly involved in the dispute and several thousand others were laid off as a consequence. Refuse was not collected, local authority services were disrupted and, for the first time, the general public witnessed demonstrations of low-paid workers across the country arguing for an improvement in their pay and conditions of work.

From early on, some local authorities, particularly those which were Labour controlled,

had urged support for the manual workers' demands. By October, more than forty councils had either expressed a willingness to engage in further talks or had said that they favoured meeting the trade unions' demands. Barking in London and Harlow in Essex agreed to pay the full fifty-five shillings claim, and by the end of October no less than twenty-five authorities had agreed to meet the claim in full. In the meantime, a detachment of Grenadier Guards and Royal Engineers had been sent in to clear up rubbish, following a request from Tower Hamlets. The Home Secretary had warned that troops might have to be brought in to ensure that the safe and effective operation of certain sewage works would be maintained.

When a further offer from the employers in late October was again turned down by the unions, it was agreed that an independent committee of enquiry should be established. In all, the strike lasted almost six weeks and was eventually resolved by the recommendations of the enquiry, chaired by Sir Jack Scamp and assisted by Professor Hugh Clegg of Warwick University and Norman Sloane, a Scottish QC who was Chairman of the Shipbuilders and Repairers National Association.

The enquiry reported on 5 November and recommended some improvement on the employers' last offer. In making their recommendations, for an additional two pounds and ten shillings per week, improved holidays and shift pay, the enquiry members added that, in the circumstances of high inflation in the country as a whole, it would be quite wrong for a smaller pay increase for low paid local authority workers to be implemented, in the vain hope that this in itself would be of more general benefit. Both sides accepted the report and the Council workers returned to work.

The response of the Heath government was to dismiss the Scamp enquiry recommendations as 'blatant nonsense' and, subsequently, Hugh Clegg, who was alleged to have been responsible for some of the key wording in the report, did not have his term of office renewed as Chairman of the Civil Service Arbitration Tribunal when it ran out the following year.

LESSONS AND IMPLICATIONS

NUPE's first major national dispute carried many implications which were to influence the union and its development for at least the next fifteen years. First, the strike itself was official, in contrast with the typical British strike at that time which was unofficial and had drawn so much critical attention from politicians, the press and employers.

Secondly, it was national and nationally led, with the leadership of the union exerting strong influence upon the deployment of action and the encouragement of local initiatives. This aspect alone underscored the importance to NUPE of clear analysis, and it emphasised the need for a sure grasp of strategy as well as the significance of reliable organisation for the widest possible mobilisation of membership support.

Thirdly, it drew many men and women into the arena of industrial disputes for the first time. Few of them had any experience of how to run strikes, including such practical questions as organising the distribution of strike pay, running a picket line, printing leaflets and gathering local support. They were quickly on to a steep learning curve, made all the more essential by the fact that hitherto NUPE's pay negotiations had largely been conducted at national level, and had mainly involved full-time officials and employers' representatives.

Fourthly, many of the workers drawn for the first time into dispute were female, the great majority of whom worked on a part-time basis and whose own rates of pay and conditions of service were considerably worse than those of their colleagues. Women members were to feature more and more prominently in NUPE's development in the next twenty years and the 1970 dispute marked a watershed for many of them.

Fifthly, NUPE's strike ushered in a long period of public service and public sector disputes, in which not only was the defence of

6 Confidence is developed by a widening understanding of, and participation in, union affairs. These are precisely the points made in a number of the 'General Conclusions' in this paper. The key factor is a rapid and widespread extension of Union Stewards and Branch (or Stewards) Committees as set out in the Executive Council Statement contained in the Union Steward's Handbook. This is necessary not merely in anticipation of any future strike situation but in order to ensure that the Union is able to maintain current levels of membership growth, adequately service members, effectively engage in local bargaining, meet the conditions likely to be created by new legislation on industrial relations and to meet the expectations of active members.

The immediate needs can therefore be summarised as:
  i.   the election of Union Stewards in every workplace and the establishment of Branch (or Stewards) Committees in every Branch;
  ii. the development of an effective system of Steward training;
  iii. the development of an effective communications system to and from Union Stewards.

By concentrating attention on these three inter-related areas the Union will be building on the success of the strike and constructing a machine capable of meeting the demands most likely to be made on the Union in the future. 9

Paper by Bernard Dix and Jack May at the Ruskin Conference of the Executive Council and Full-time Officers, January 1971

' The rapid growth in the number of Union Stewards in recent years is an indication of the fundamental changes taking place within the Union, and it rests on a number of considerations. The first is the need to establish and maintain an efficient line of communications within a large organisation which is growing every day. The second is the increasing complexity of the kind of negotiations which can only be conducted at the level of the workplace. The third is the need to offset the attempts of the Government - through the Industrial Relations Bill - to drive a legislative wedge between Stewards and other Union representatives, such as full-time Officials and the Executive Council. Last, but by no means least, is the philosophical consideration; the need to continually expand the democratic base of the Union through an organisational framework which extends from the individual member at work to the Executive Council in a continuous process of decision making.

There is one further aspect of the need to continue to build our system of Union Stewards. As the Union has grown we have added to our staff and full-time officials in order to maintain a high level of personal service to members. We shall continue this process, but if we are to improve the level of service it is essential that there should be a greater integration of work, and a sharing of responsibility, between full-time Officials, Stewards and Branch Officers. Our ultimate aim must be to remove any feelings of 'us' and 'them' in the Union and to arrive at a situation where there is complete acceptance that we are all members of the same organisation performing our own particular jobs in the common interests of all the members. '

Bob Pinchin, presidential address to the 1971 Conference of NUPE

their standards of living and working conditions in question, but also the whole role and future of the public services themselves. Increasingly, as manufacturing industry went into decline, and new duties were imposed upon local authorities and the National Health Service, so employment in the public services expanded. At the same time, successive governments were keen to impose limits upon the costs of the public services, particularly pay costs, given the importance of earnings in the total cost of service provision.

Finally, and probably most importantly, the conduct of the dispute, consisting of a rolling programme of selective industrial action, not only made less demands upon the union for strike pay, but also proved unpredictable and disruptive for employers. It also presented problems of local union organisation and branch level activity for NUPE itself.

Reflecting on the lessons of the strike in early 1971, Bernard Dix and Jack May, the union's National Local Government Officer, drew attention to the need for the union quickly to develop its emerging system of local union stewards. Throughout the dispute, the value of local organisation and the activity of branch level members had proved

invaluable. It was evident that dependence upon full-time officials and branch secretaries alone would not be sufficient to sustain such sophisticated forms of activity and to maintain organisation and morale amongst members and fellow trade unionists at the same time as winning support from the public generally.

Thus it was that, building upon the 1970 dispute and the national development of union steward organisation, NUPE began a series of changes which were to have far-reaching implications for the union's own systems of organisation, democracy and representation. A key figure in these developments was Bernard Dix, who, in his brilliant partnership with Alan Fisher, provided the intellectual drive and imagination for many of NUPE's initiatives. Schooled in the Young Communist League and the National Council of Labour Colleges, and a fluent journalist, Dix brought powerful analytical and strategic skills to the service of the union and, in particular, to his close friend and colleague Alan Fisher. Throughout the 1970s, these two were to help shape not only NUPE's tactics in a wide variety of campaigns, but also the very development of NUPE itself.

9. Strengthening the union

UNION STEWARDS

Despite earlier hesitancy the development of a system of union stewards for NUPE can be traced back into the 1950s and before. Most branches at that time had so-called 'collecting stewards', who went round each month to persuade, cajole or otherwise induce members to pay up their union subscriptions. In conducting this work, they were brought into close contact with NUPE's widely dispersed membership and were able to pass on information both ways, forming a key link between members at large, the branch officials and NUPE's paid officers. But, towards the end of the 1960s, agreements were increasingly concluded with employers to replace manual collections with deduction of trade union subscriptions at source, and the old role of the collecting stewards fell into disuse.

At the same time, some groups of workers, notably in the ambulance service and refuse collection, had already developed an ele-

mentary system of shop steward organisation, not unlike that found in manufacturing industry, particularly engineering. In 1969 a national agreement gave recognition to stewards and NUPE was amongst a number of unions in the public services which began rapidly to develop a system of union stewards. The local government agreement was followed two years later, in 1971, by a similar recognition agreement for union stewards in the National Health Service. In 1971, the union issued its first union steward's handbook for the health service.

However, despite the fact that NUPE's steward system was to expand rapidly in the 1970s, it was not achieved without some opposition. Bryn Roberts himself had vehemently argued that the principal issue of British trade union organisation was not more shop steward development, which he warned would lead to an 'epidemic of industrial troubles', but rather greater commit-

A TUC delegation meets Prime Minister Margaret Thatcher in October 1980 to discuss the economy. With Alan Fisher (left) are Clive Jenkins (ASTMS), Tom Jackson (Post Office Workers), Geoffrey Drain (NALGO), and Norman Willis (TUC Deputy General Secretary).

HULTON DEUTCH COLLECTION

Strengthening the union **93**

Alan Fisher speaks at a rally for jobs in Cardiff in July 1981.
PAT MANTLE

accurate, this meant that NUPE then had one union steward for every fifty-nine members (in 1936, the union had one collector for every thirty members). In 1974 only 29 per cent of the union stewards in post had held the position for four years or more and 59 per cent said that the members they represented had not been represented by a union steward before they had taken up office.

According to a detailed study carried out in the early 1980s, almost two thirds of NUPE's local government branches reported that union stewards were first introduced between 1970 and 1978. Three quarters of them reported that all sections of the NUPE-organised workforce were covered by stewards, even if this was not always from the immediate workgroup itself. By 1981, a NUPE Executive Council discussion document was claiming that the union had no less than 25,000 stewards. Still, it suggested, there were difficulties 'in getting a steward elected at each workplace who, moreover, is willing to undertake training and do more than just pass on information to member.'

THE ANCILLARY WORKERS' DISPUTE, 1972-73

Workplace and local organisation was soon to receive a further burst of support in the conduct of Britain's first national industrial dispute in the National Health Service. Once again, the twin triggers for the action were the appallingly low pay of NUPE and other trade unions' members amongst hospital ancillary workers, and a Government-imposed incomes policy. In November 1972 the Conservative government introduced a ninety day freeze on all pay settlements, thus breaking the link with the union's local authority members, who had settled for two pounds forty pence immediately before the freeze was announced. At the end of the freeze period, the Government indicated that 'Stage Two' of their policy would impose a statutory limit on all pay increases of an additional 'one pound plus four per cent'. Quite remarkably, the Government sought partial justification for its actions by claiming that the policy would be particularly beneficial to low paid workers!

Just as local government manual workers had been plunged headlong into their first

ment to the rationalisation of trade union structures along the lines of industrial unionism. Some branch secretaries were also reluctant to see shop stewards introduced formally into the branch. Opponents argued that they would do very little more than operate as 'post boxes', perfectly able to stir up and unearth difficulties but rarely able to resolve them. This would simply result in additional workloads for branch secretaries themselves, and the frustration of membership expectations which had been falsely aroused by the stewards.

Despite this, the growth of stewards continued. In 1970, 39 per cent of the union's 1600 branches had no union stewards, but this had dropped to only 11 per cent by 1974. An estimate at the end of 1973 suggested that the union had just over 7000 stewards, of whom 19 per cent were women. If the estimates were

taste of strike action two years earlier, now it was the turn of the lowest paid section of the NHS labour force. Under the slogan 'hospital workers demand justice', a nation-wide campaign was launched by NUPE, culminating first in a one-day protest day of action on 13 December 1972. According to estimates, more than 50,000 marched in various towns and cities in support of the ancillaries and a further 100,000 took part in stoppages of work. The day of action was followed up by a ballot of union members, in which 79 per cent of NUPE's branches voted in favour of industrial action of one kind or another. The four unions represented on the Ancillary Staffs Council agreed that action would begin on 1 March 1973 and would include a mixture of widespread selective strikes, non-co-operation, restrictions on hospital admissions and lightning walk-outs.

By the end of the first week of action, more than 750 hospitals were affected by the dispute. Almost 10,000 hospital beds were out of action nationwide, and by the third week in March this had grown to almost 30,000. For the first time ever, the average number of working days lost per 1000 employees through strike action was greater in the NHS than in British industry as a whole. In the course of the dispute, two pickets were arrested in London for obstruction and they were subsequently welcomed as heroes by the union's National Conference in May at Eastbourne.

RANK AND FILE ACTIVITY

Alongside national and official sponsorship of union stewards, there was also evidence of unofficial 'rank and file' activity at workplace level, often supported by individual NUPE full-time officers. These initiatives multiplied as pressure mounted for action in the NHS. Unofficial action soon spawned a series of radical and lively news sheets and journals with titles such as *Red Alert, Germ's Eye View, Needle* and *Reds in Medicine*. Across the country, local militancy in NUPE and the TGWU especially had already produced a small rash of unofficial disputes. By the time the national leadership of NUPE was ready to call for action amongst ancillary workers, unofficial networks of members, stewards and political activists were already in place, ready to push

Bernard Dix speaking on behalf of the Labour Party Executive at the 1981 Labour Party Conference.
SHEILA GRAY

the union as far as it would go.

Most influential of the groups which sprung up was LASH, the London alliance of shop stewards for health workers, established in October 1972 with its own journal entitled *Backlash*. Soon to be transformed into a national unofficial alliance (NASH), the group was deeply influenced by political activists from groups such as the International Socialists, the International Marxist Group, and Workers' Fight. Amongst the demands of NASH – and their call soon spread – was the abolition of private practice within the NHS. As the dispute gained momentum, the practical focus of this demand became the ending of all pay beds in NHS hospitals.

As well as adding an explicit political dimension to the pay claim of ancillary workers, NASH and its associated groupings also declared openly against 'the petty and fac-

The introduction of private contractors in the public services provoked a series of disputes including a long battle in Tory controlled Wandsworth. Here members of the Wandsworth strike committee display the union's message in April 1982. CARLOS AUGUSTO / IFL

tional barriers' existing between unions and occupations in health. They pointed out that, in their view, low pay was partly predicated on keeping wage costs in the NHS down by the even greater exploitation of migrant workers and women. In any case, they took the view that the unions' official pay claim for four pounds was far too low and ought to be doubled. Nor were the Government and employers the only villains of the piece: 'we often have two battles on our hands - against the bosses and against male union officials.'

This time the Government and the chief minister involved, Sir Keith Joseph, were not going to be drawn into supporting any inquiry favoured by the trade unions, whether independent or not. The Government urged the unions to take their case to its newly established Pay Board, operating within a strict pay code, which was due to report on 'anomalies' in September. The unions refused the offer.

As the dispute extended into its sixth week, it became evident that NUPE required a way forward, or a way out that meant that the union did not lose face, that the employers' offer should not be sanctioned, that the support of NUPE's activists could be maintained and that the actions of its ancillary members could be vindicated. As on many such occasions, it was Bernard Dix who provide a sophisticated analysis and a range of options for the union's Executive Council to consider. Following the Executive Council debate, the dispute was ended in April and the ancillary staffs were awarded two pounds per week for males and one pound eighty pence for women. Although the pay claim had been far

Olwen Davies from Neath became the first woman President of NUPE in 1982.
DENIS DORAN

from fully met, NUPE had taken a further, major step in its development. Industrial relations in the NHS were never to be the same again and change in NUPE itself had been further advanced.

REORGANISATION

At the same time as facing severe problems on the wages front, NUPE and all the other trade unions in local government, the health service and water were confronted by wholesale reorganisation of the services. Planned to be implemented in 1973-74, the administrative boundaries, responsibilities and management arrangements in the services were all radically altered. For NUPE's Executive Council and National Conference, this

❝ We have been concerned to establish a general pay level that we judge to be appropriate for nurses in relation to other groups both inside the NHS and elsewhere. We are aware that nurses' pay generally has fallen behind others at comparable levels of income since the April 1970 review.

We are in no doubt that the pay of nurses and midwives has fallen behind other occupations and professions which, four years ago, were at broadly similar income levels, and it is important that this should be remedied... Whilst we do not believe that, whatever the level of pay, men and women would enter the profession solely for the monetary rewards provided, we regard it as essential that the vocational nature of the job should not lead to undervaluation of it in financial terms. ❞

The Report of the Committee of Inquiry into the Pay and Related Conditions of Service of Nurses and Midwives (The 'Halsbury' Report), 1974

During 1982 health service workers took action in support of the
claim for a 12 per cent increase
in pay – culminating in a
national demonstration in
September. During the dispute,
Sean Geraghty, a print worker,
was imprisoned for action in
support of the health workers.

SARAH SAUNDERS / PHOTO CO-OP

seemed an excellent opportunity to review
their own structures and organisation. The
union took the unprecedented step of com-
missioning an academic study of all the
union's operations, from the Department of
Sociology at the University of Warwick.

The timescale was short: the research had
to be completed between July 1973 and August 1974. Upon receipt of the study, which
would be sent out unaltered and in full to the
union's branches, the Executive would make
its own recommendations to a Special National Conference early in 1975. The three
researchers quickly got down to work, visiting
branches, area conferences, workplace meetings and discussions with NUPE members
and officers all over the country. They conducted a number of surveys and were given
open access to union papers and documents.
All of this took place against a background,
not only of the ancillary dispute and reorganisation of the services, but also in the
wider context of vigorous debate about the
future organisation of NUPE itself. Added to
this were the normal day-to-day activities of a
growing union, itself at the centre of turbulent industrial relations and challenges to
public policy.

A TURBULENT PERIOD

As the oil and economic crisis deepened,
Heath's government was successively challenged in the political, industrial and social
arenas. Its attempts radically to reform labour
relations by use of the law and the courts
were already in chaos when it became locked
in a desperate struggle with the country's
miners for the second time in less than two
years. After declaring first a State of Emergency and then the 'three day week', Edward
Heath raised the stakes sharply by seeking a
general election on the basis of 'who runs the
country, the Government or the miners?'
Whatever the answer, it was made clear in the
election results that it was no longer to be the
Conservative Party. A minority Labour government was returned to power and a new
approach was instigated to labour law and to
relations with the unions, embraced in the
Social Contract.

However, Labour's election to office did
not ease the enormous pressures which had
built up on the wages front. When the nurses' pay settlement was published, it was not
long before the nurses took their protests to
the streets, for the first time ever. Nurses
from NUPE, COHSE and NALGO, together

even with the non TUC- affiliated Royal College of Nursing, mounted a series of marches, demonstrations, protest rallies and some selective action in the early summer of 1974. It was only when Barbara Castle, the new Labour Secretary of State for Health announced an inquiry, to be chaired by Lord Halsbury, that the action died down.

THE WARWICK REPORT

In August 1974, the researchers delivered their report on NUPE's structure. Entitled *Organisation and Change in the National Union of Public Employees*, it soon became known as the 'Warwick Report'.

The researchers' recommendations covered the whole of the union, from workplace and branch level through to the organisation of the union nationally. Its five principal themes, however, were clear. First, the union should concentrate on developing its internal systems of democracy, participation and accountability. This would mean strengthening its system of union stewards, encouraging more workplace and sectional meetings and making lay members less dependent upon full-time officers for routine matters of organisation and representation.

Secondly, levels of decision-making throughout the union should be linked together, providing opportunities for members to influence policy at all levels. Thirdly, greater recognition should be given to representation of staff in the different services in which NUPE members were working.

Fourthly, there should be more devolved authority and initiative to NUPE's Divisions at regional level. Fifthly, and most radically, the union should implement special arrangements for the representation of women members on the union's Executive Council and new Divisional level structures. This would mean introducing reserved seats with the intention of underpinning and boosting women's representation in NUPE.

All of the principles were accepted by the Executive Council and the great majority of the detailed recommendations were also supported. The Executive produced its own report and recommendations and these were considered by delegates at a Special National Conference convened in Manchester in January 1975, specifically to deal with the Warwick Report and Executive Council recommendations.

In line with the approach of the Executive

NUPE water workers on a one day strike in October 1982 in support of a pay claim at the Beckton Sewage Works where Albin Taylor had worked and organised in the 1890s.

Barking Hospital cleaners on strike against their employers, the private contractor Crothalls, join a miners' picket line at the West Drayton coal depot in June 1984. RICHARD GILBERT / IFL

NUPE members at Highbury help register a resounding 'Yes' vote in the political fund ballot, 1985.
JUDY HARRISON

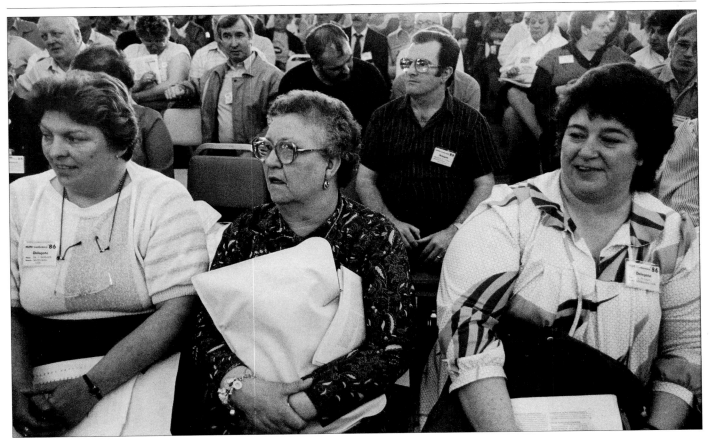

Council, the Special Conference delegates accepted the recommendations and NUPE embarked on a wholesale and long-term re-organisation of its structures. At the heart of these developments was their commitment to greater membership participation in the affairs of the union, especially for its female members, who already constituted over two-thirds of the union's members, giving NUPE the single largest group of women trade unionists in the country.

CUTS AND THE SOCIAL CONTRACT

Scarcely had NUPE embarked upon the re-structuring of its organisation, than it found itself once more in conflict with government policy. This time, the issue was not simply low pay and general restrictions upon the public services, it had to do with the whole of government economic and social policy. The only difference was that, this time, NUPE's opposition was to the Labour government.

The origins of NUPE's campaign dated from its response to the government's proposals set out in the White Paper, *The Attack on Inflation*, presented to Parliament in the heat of the economic crisis of July 1975. This documented the terms of the six pound pay limit agreed with the TUC and, remarkably, included an extract from the TUC's own pub-

A scene from the 1986 local government sectional conference.
PHILIP WOLMUTH

❡ In evaluating our suggestions for the future structure of NUPE a number of fundamental considerations should be borne in mind. Union reorganisation means more than just a change of rules, important though this is. It extends to the very attitudes and philosophy underlying the Union's overall structure. This is the meaning of references in the report to the 'character' and 'logic' of the Union. Not every single challenge and problem that trade unions face can be resolved by changes in structure alone. We referred earlier to the importance of policy and sense of purpose in trade unions. Furthermore, some challenges need to be met by more than the policies and structure of any individual trade union: they call for action and determination by the working class and their organisations as a whole. ❡

Organisation and Change in the National Union of Public Employees, Bob Fryer, Andy Fairclough and Tom Manson

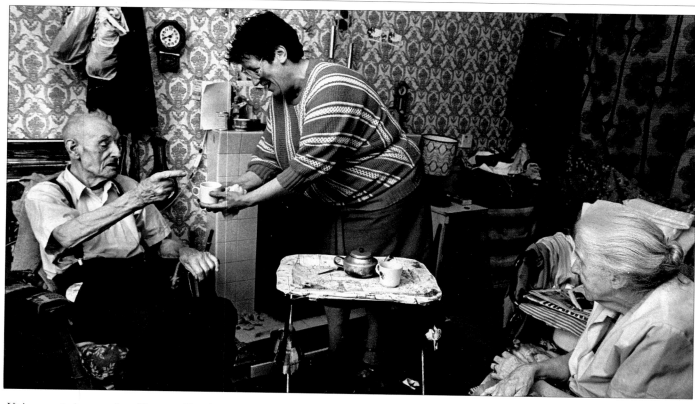

JOANNE O'BRIEN / FORMAT

Union campaigns against Tory cuts highlighted the value of public services to the community. Many of these caring jobs are undertaken by women, who by the 1980s made up more than two-thirds of NUPE's membership. Here a home help in Belfast helps clients – both in their nineties.

lication, *The Development of the Social Contract.*

In response to the government, NUPE published its own document, entitled *Inflation: Attack or Retreat?*, which argued that a proper recognition of union responsibility for maintaining a Labour government in office implied a duty to oppose 'short term palliatives' and to suggest instead a comprehensive set of alternative policies designed to deal with what the union identified as 'deep rooted faults in the economy'.

Throughout the country, union branches and shop stewards' committees formed organisational links to fight back against the cuts. Joint union committees organised their own meetings, demonstrations, pickets and lobbies all over the country.

In advance of the 1976 April budget, NUPE again produced its own 'economic review' entitled, *Time to Change Course,* once more calling for 'a radical interventionist industrial policy' to deal with the 'deep-seated nature of the structural problems of the economy'. In the absence of such a change of direction, NUPE proposed to confront the Government with the possibility of a general trade union retreat from an 'involvement in wages policy' (to which NUPE was already opposed in 1975). If the Government cut standards of living and left only the channel of collective bargaining for unions to protect

their members, then the sole route open to unions would be to seek compensatory wage increases.

This was not the approach NUPE preferred; the union advocated instead a long list of programmes organised under four main heads: an immediate attack on unemployment through a selective reflation of the economy; the introduction of socialist planning measures; an end to the attack on public services; and social measures to reduce the impact of inflation on working people and to redistribute income and wealth. These demands were repeated by the union's General Secretary at the Special TUC in June 1976, where he also pointed out the dangers inherent in the social contract dialogues with the Government. He argued that trade unionists could become 'mesmerised by the process' and fail to appreciate the power of 'international capital' and the threat of 'incorporation in the apparatus of the state'.

At the same time, NUPE was continuing its joint meetings with NALGO at national level within which the possibility of a common approach to the government's policy of cuts was raised. The Executive Council of NUPE had also endorsed in April two resolutions from different sections of the union; one called for 'a massive campaign of publicity opposing the Government's present policy on public expenditure cuts', including 'organising public protests and demonstrations, where possible, with other unions and pressure groups'; and the other for 'a mass lobby of Parliament in conjunction with other sympathetic organisations to demand a reversal in the present government policy'. Acceptance of these policies for the union coincided with the Government's proposals about Phase Two of its social contract incomes policy and the TUC response, the special TUC congress and a meeting of general secretaries in public service unions. A letter was also received by the NUPE Executive Council from the civil service unions, the CPSA and SCPS, expressing a desire to be associated with a NUPE campaign against the cuts.

For NUPE, discussion at the level of the Executive focussed around five issues: (i) how to combat the apparent division in the labour movement generally over public expenditure such as that exemplified by the recent speech by Hugh Scanlon (AUEW) recognising the need for cuts; (ii) how to build unity within the government/public sector/public service unions; (iii) how to mobilise the membership and build upon membership action against the cuts and against the hospital closures stemming from the inter-regional reallocation of resources in the NHS; (iv) how to reconcile the union's response to the Government's Phase Two proposals (and TUC response) with the union's overall policy set out in *Time to Change Course* and; (v) how best to plan the mass lobby of Parliament.

The NUPE mass lobby of Parliament was initially planned to coincide with a lobby being prepared for early November 1976 by the TUC Southern Region, including a rally in Central Hall Westminster. Union information and propaganda circulars were distributed to branches and resolutions were prepared for the TUC and Labour Party Conferences. A joint meeting between the entire NALGO and NUPE research staffs was held to discuss practical co-operation in the campaign against public expenditure cuts and a special meeting of the NALGO/NUPE joint committee was arranged to explore an approach to other unions about a joint lobby of Parliament. NUPE itself organised for lobbies of the TUC at Brighton and the Labour Party Conference in Blackpool as a build-up to the November Parliamentary lobby.

The mass lobby of Parliament took place on 17 November 1976 and from it developed the joint union National Steering Committee against the Cuts. Part of the work of building official unity at national trade union level had been associated with another campaign, concerning private practice in the National Health Service, culminating in a joint statement distributed at the TUC by five trade unions - ASTMS, COHSE, GMWU, NALGO and NUPE (*Private Practice has no place in the NHS*).

On the day of the mass lobby, estimates of the numbers of trade unionists taking part in the demonstration ranged from 40,000 to 80,000 and it was claimed to be the largest weekday demonstration in London since before the Second World War. In some places,

> ❛ The centralized and concentrated NUPE was facing a growing workload from rapid membership growth, productivity bargaining and the reorganization of local government and health service. If they continued with the same system of decision-making and did not considerably increase the number of FTOs, there would be a reduction in the level of service to the members. This course would not have helped NUPE in its attempts to remain economically and industrially viable in a highly competitive union environment in which the trade-off between subscriptions and services is a crucial factor in joining one union rather than another, particularly in the lower paid areas covered by NUPE. Thus, as in the case of the TGWU, an ideological commitment to greater democracy combined with issues of economy and effectiveness to persuade the leadership and the FTOs to choose the other strategy, which was increasing lay involvement and participation in the bargaining process. ❜
>
> *Change in Trade Unions*, R. Undy, V. Ellis, W.E.J. McCarthy and A.M. Halmos

*NUPE's delegation to the
1987 TUC.*

J. SMITH / PROFILE PHOTO AGENCY

one day strikes were held to coincide with the lobby and special trains and buses brought thousands of rank and file unionists into London to register their opposition to the Government's policy of public expenditure cuts.

In the wake of the massive demonstration, a meeting of General Secretaries and National Officers was held under the auspices of the National Steering Committee. It decided (i) to re-establish the Steering Committee on a continuing basis; (ii) to hold further meetings of senior full-time officials of unions; (iii) to initiate a further stage of the campaign, including regional 'days of action' of stoppages, demonstrations and lobbies; (iv) to establish regional and local joint union committees; (v) to explore the possibility of a delegate conference on the Social Wage; and (vi) to prepare and publish joint literature setting out the arguments against the cuts and the case for the alternative strategy. Within such a strategy, particular attention was to be given not to create the impression that the constituent unions were attempting to organise a mini-TUC or alternative to the TUC. It was further agreed that each union should keep the others informed of its data collection and policy statements. NUPE, as the initiating body, would continue to provide the secre-

tary of the National Steering Committee.

Throughout late 1976 and the early months of 1977, local demonstrations and days of action took place, often with strong local support from 'non-member' unions of the Steering Committee (e.g. British Leyland shop stewards in Birmingham). Local struggles and campaigns (especially in the NHS) drew some strength from the general ambience of official opposition to the Government's strategy, although particular struggles were always threatened by their isolation. In March, the national delegate conference on the Social Wage took place in central London, attended by 200 delegates from twenty-three different unions. Although called to discuss the social wage, the conference ranged widely, discussing the positive contribution public expenditure could make to fight the crisis of working class unemployment and falling standards of living, as well as to the 'rejuvenation' of the economy.

WAGES STRATEGY AND THE 'WINTER OF DISCONTENT'

Throughout the 1970s, NUPE's case for the development of a united labour movement policy on low pay had been voiced with greater and greater determination, at its own conferences, in the TUC and with the

104   *A Century of Service*

*Rodney Bickerstaffe, NUPE
General Secretary since 1982
addresses the 1988 Labour
Party Conference.*

STEFANO CAGNONI

Alan Fisher, who was General Secretary from 1968-82, sadly died in March 1988. He had been suffering from leukaemia. He presided over the union during its great period of expansion, democratic development and movement into a prominent position in British industrial relations.

At a memorial meeting held in Friends House tributes were paid by, amongst others, Norman Willis General Secretary of the TUC, Michael Foot, and his friend and journalist Keith Harper. Bernard Dix summed up Alan's life with NUPE succinctly:

❛ The history of NUPE can never be separated from the history of Alan Fisher, the history of Alan Fisher can never be separated from the history of NUPE. ❜

Tom Sawyer, Deputy General Secretary since 1982, became a prominent member of the Labour Party National Executive during the 1980s. Here he listens to Barbara Castle at the 1988 Labour Party Conference.

Labour Party in government as well as in opposition. The union's approach had brought it into sharp conflict, not just with employers and governments, but also with some colleague unions, especially in manufacturing. Even so, the leadership of the union was clear as to its primary duties: those were to defend the pay, conditions and jobs of its members and, in so doing, also to fight on behalf of the country's public services.

So it was that in March 1978 the Executive Council started down a pathway that was eventually to lead it and other public service unions into perhaps the most talked about, if little analysed, dispute of its existence. Building on its earlier policy statements and publications, the Executive Council produced its document *Union Wages Strategy 1978-79.* The report set out in some detail the history of wage settlements in the 1970s for its two largest groups of workers, council manual workers and hospital ancillaries. Even taking into account the beneficial effects of the flat-rate six pound pay increase of the Social Contract, the Executive noted that 'a very disturbing feature of the period since 1970 is the extent to which the relative earnings position of manual workers in local government and the NHS has become substantially worse

in relation to average earnings.'

The union's main recommendation, subsequently endorsed by its 1978 national conference, was to mount an immediate and vigourous campaign. It was planned to concentrate on winning support in four main areas: amongst NUPE's own membership; in the wider labour movement, for policies designed to eliminate low pay; with other unions and the TUC, to agree a joint, practical approach to pay bargaining; and to achieve public support for the union's campaigns against low pay and in favour of NUPE's alternative economic strategy.

Already, the embattled Labour government, now under the leadership of Jim Callaghan, had failed to win trade union endorsement for the next steps in its attack on inflation, including particularly a tightening of recommended limits on pay increases first to 10 per cent and then to 5 per cent. All the signs, as usual, were that public sector pay would be used both as an example and as a regulator for the rest of the economy. As the NUPE policy statement put it, 'the clear implication is that the Government expects the local authority manual workers' settlement in November to be modest.' The unions' claim, for both local government and health, was

for an increase of 40 per cent, from forty-two pounds fifty pence to sixty pounds.

The employers' response to both claims was to offer 5 per cent, which was immediately rejected. Industrial action began with a one day public services strike and mass demonstration in London on 22 January. Full-scale strike action across the country quickly followed, with officials from NUPE and the other unions concerned striving to maintain the provision of essential emergency services. By the beginning of February, the DHSS announced that approximately half the hospitals in England and Wales were operating

emergency services only and that ambulance staffs were responding only to emergency calls. Nor was the union only in dispute with the Government and public service employers; throughout the winter residential workers in a Cheshire home were engaged in a bitter struggle over dismissals, eventually resolved after a committee of enquiry.

In a series of meetings involving union leaders, representatives of the TUC, employers and government ministers, great anxiety was expressed about the escalation of action. Once more, refuse was not collected, remaining heaped up in the streets and

Nottingham ambulance staff during the national dispute of 1989-90.

JOHN BIRDSALL PHOTOGRAPHY

❝ In 1977 the Royal Commission on the Press published its findings and on the crucial question of press bias against the labour movement; the majority report concluded 'that industrial relations matters are presented in the national press predominantly in terms of disputes; that reports themselves are highly factual and lack overt bias…'

In 1979 the popular press coverage of the lorry drivers and public sector workers' strike destroys any credibility in the Royal Commission's conclusions that reports are factual and unbiased…

The popular press usually present strikers not as average decent working men and women but as selfish, callous militants hell bent on intimidation and violence. Strikes, or rather the popular press, throw up heroes and villains and the lorry drivers and public sector workers provided plenty of both. ❞

Never Mind the Qualities Read the Myths, Labour Research, April 1979

squares, and the press abounded with scare stories about threats to public health from rats and vermin. In a story which gained greatly in embellishment over the following years, it was alleged that Liverpool grave-diggers (members, apparently, not of NUPE but of the GMWU) had callously refused grieving relatives the right to bury their dead.

The subsequent intransigence of the NUPE leadership, in refusing to accept or recommend inadequate compromise offers from the government and employers, was overwhelmingly supported by NUPE health members in a ballot. In another ballot result announced in early March, all four unions representing local authority workers, including NUPE, accepted the latest offer from the employers.

This latest, and most bitter, dispute between some of Britain's lowest paid workers and the state placed NUPE in the unenviable spotlight of press and Tory outrage. The focus ought rather to have been the clumsy miscalculations of the Callaghan government, which ultimately led to its downfall, General Election defeat and the return of the first Thatcher government.

With another almost uncanny, gross lack of timing only days before its humiliating demise, in February 1979 the Labour government established an Independent Standing Commission on Pay Comparability. The first groups to be examined were NHS ancillaries, ambulance staffs, university manual workers and local authority manuals. Just to add a further ironic twist, with the Government helping history to repeat itself, only this time as tragedy, the Commission was to be chaired by Professor Hugh Clegg, whose role

in settling the first dirty jobs dispute had cost him a job at the hands of Edward Heath.

Thus, in part, was born the mythology of the so-called 'Winter of Discontent'. In all, three and a quarter million working days were lost through the public service workers' strike in 1979. This was just 11 per cent of the total lost through stoppages in the same year. The lorry drivers' dispute, in January, had accounted for a further 900,000 days of stoppages, but neither the drivers nor the public service strikers came anywhere near the almost 18 million days lost in engineering in 1979, some 61 per cent of the total. Popular 'memory' recalled a very different story, assiduously fed as it was by lurid references in the press and political propaganda.

Interestingly enough, in one of the very few independent accounts of the period, Eric Wigham, an ex-Labour correspondent of *The Times* newspaper, and by no stretch of the imagination an uncritical supporter of the unions, saw things rather differently:

> From the political point of view the local government and health service stoppages were disastrous for Labour. The media were full of stories of what seemed callousness in the treatment of hospital patients and others. More economically damaging was a month's strike of some 65,000 lorry drivers which began on 2 January and was accompanied by widespread picketing of factories and ports and resulted in the laying off of 20,000 non-driver employees and an estimated 250,000 workers in other industries. Reports of violence and mass picketing of undertakings which had nothing to do with the dispute aroused much public criticism.

10. The Thatcher years and after

National demonstration in support of the health workers dispute, September 1982.

A. NICOLA

SUSTAINED ATTACK

From 1979 onwards, under four successive Conservative governments, trade unions in Britain sustained an unprecedented attack. The story is familiar enough to those who lived through it. It comprised a lethal combination of restrictive and punitive anti-union laws and the deployment of the police in industrial disputes. It entailed the destruction of almost three million jobs in manufacturing and the deliberate use of unemployment to attempt to regulate the economy (and the subsequent fiddling of the official unemployment statistics). There was wholesale privatisation of large areas of the public sector (particularly where vast private profits could follow), an assault upon the powers and functions of local government, combined with deep cuts in public expenditure, the forced

introduction of compulsory competitive tendering, and the hiving off of schools and hospitals.

In a determined effort to tear up British political consensus on the welfare state, founded on wartime agreement and the reforming drive of Attlee's post-Second World War Labour government, the Tory governments of Margaret Thatcher zealously embarked upon a programme of privatisation based on open hostility to public provision and collective organisation. There followed the wholesale restructuring of the rates system, including the introduction of the iniquitous poll tax and a tightening of restrictions on the availability of welfare benefits. There was undisguised hatred of independent trade unionism and a determination to put an end to the very idea of socialism. Key targets in

Health workers demonstration, September 1982. After the dispute at NUPE's Conference in 1983 there were renewed calls for a merger of public service unions, especially COHSE.

DENIS DORAN

this vicious crusade were the public sector in general and Labour local authorities and the NHS in particular. Where there was resistance, as in the case of the Greater London Council, or the Metropolitan Counties (set up in 1974 by a Conservative government), they were unceremoniously abolished.

Mrs Thatcher, John Major and their fellow Tory ministers were well aware that the accomplishment of such a radical programme would require more than just victory at the polls. The trade unions and their likely resistance needed to be confronted head on. The plans were laid first while the Tories were still

in opposition in 1978 and then developed, piecemeal, in the so-called 'step-by-step' approach to increasingly restrictive labour laws. Never a Party likely to forego an opportunity for vindictive revenge, the Conservatives had in their sights trade unionists in the mines, in the civil service, in public transport, in local government and in the NHS, amongst others. Along the way, with the active support of employers (and occasionally some trade unionists), devastating blows were delivered to seafarers, newspaper printers and journalists during the course of some of Britain's most bitter disputes. NUPE was at the centre

❛ I make no apology yet again for saying what many of you may well have heard but I am going to keep on saying it: it is no use Mrs. Thatcher standing at that cenotaph every November on behalf of the country honouring the dead whom we all honour. She gets no medals for honouring the dead one day a year when she dishonours the living for the next 364 days.

That is what she is doing: dishonouring the elderly who have served this country well, nine million of them, many in desperate straits. That is what she is doing to those desperate four million unemployed and to the… working poor on poverty wages. ❜

Rodney Bickerstaff at the National Conference of NUPE, May 1985

NUPE official talking to members at Moorfields Hospital.

MAGGIE MURRAY / FORMAT

of many of these struggles, either as chief protagonist or, frequently, as active supporter of the workers and their unions.

UNION MEMBERSHIP

According to official figures, by the end of 1991 total membership of British trade unions had fallen by almost four million members from its 1979 peak. Some individual unions had suffered huge drops. The TGWU had lost a million members, the Engineers had lost six hundred thousand, and estimates suggested that the NUM had lost over three hundred thousand, most of them

---

Lil Stevens from Birmingham, winner of the TUC Gold Badge in 1981 and NUPE President in 1984. On receiving the Gold Badge she said:

PHILIP WOLMUTH

❛ … it is with great pride and with a touch of humility that I accept this badge on behalf of the National Union of Public Employees and myself. It is but a small contribution that I have made to this great working class movement of outs.

In accepting this badge, it would be remiss of me to let this opportunity pass without making reference to that other female who has done so much to damage the prospects of women – Margaret Thatcher. I am a school meals lady and as a member of NUPE I have witnessed literally thousands of my colleagues, most of them who are part-time, going down the road, not to the dole for they do not qualify to be counted amongst the unemployed, but to a living standard not unlike that of the 1930s that most of us can remember. Comrades, we must fight and unite together, as the previous speaker said, or else our movement will be nothing. ❜

Miners supporting Coventry health workers in their campaign for a living wage in June 1982.
COVENTRY EVENING TELEGRAPH

after that union's year-long, heroic struggle against pit closures. By sharp contrast, the Royal College of Nursing, which remained unaffiliated to the TUC, and was the only organisation representing workers in the public services to be invited to meet the Prime Minister in Downing Street, increased its membership by over one hundred thousand, reaching a total of just under three hundred thousand by the end of 1991.

In all of these circumstances, NUPE's relatively small reduction in numbers by some 170,000, down to 551,000 at the end of 1991, was a remarkable achievement. Continued attention to the recruitment and retention of members, improved membership services, vigourous campaigns on behalf of the low paid, the NHS, local government and the public services generally, all contributed to NUPE's resistance to precipitous decline.

PARADOX

Indeed, there was something of a paradox about the fortunes of NUPE in the Thatcher

NUPE on the march.
GINA GLOVER / PHOTO CO-OP

years and after. In a period in which trade unionism was facing its most difficult times since the General Strike of 1926, NUPE began to see the partial realisation of some of its most cherished ambitions. First, there was the union's growing stature inside the TUC. After its colourful General Secretary Bryn Roberts had been deliberately kept off the General Council of the TUC throughout his period of office, twice within a decade two of his successors had become Presidents of the TUC.

The first was Alan Fisher, who held the office from 1980-81, a year before he retired from NUPE. In sharp contrast to the fortunes of Roberts, Fisher was a member of the General Council throughout the time that he was NUPE's General Secretary, from 1968 to 1982. He was succeeded in 1982 by Rodney Bickerstaffe, who, like Alan Fisher before him, had worked for the union since completing his education. 'Bick', as he is known to members of his family and close friends, became TUC President in 1991. He also be-

Home help, Belfast.
JOANNE O'BRIEN / FORMAT

came a widely respected Chair of one of its senior committees, the Economic Committee, was a frequent commentator on the radio and television about trade union and economic affairs and represented the TUC on the European TUC (ETUC).

NUPE's second achievement of the period was its growing influence in, and importance to, the Labour Party. In a unique combination, the post of Chairman of the Labour Party was also held from 1990-91 by another newly promoted senior officer of the union, Tom Sawyer, who became NUPE's first-ever Deputy General Secretary in 1982 when the senior officer structure was amended after the retirement of Bernard Dix. Like his col-

league 'Bick' at the TUC, Tom quickly became an influential member of the Labour Party NEC. As the joint successors to the earlier partnership of Fisher and Dix, Rodney Bickerstaffe and Tom Sawyer rapidly established themselves as passionate and eloquent voices on behalf of NUPE, the public service workers and the merits of the labour movement generally.

LOW PAY

A third notable success for NUPE, in this otherwise difficult period, was the union's achievement in securing support for its policy in favour of a statutory minimum wage from both the Labour Party and the TUC. In

❝ We have a moral crusade. It is our moral crusade to do something for the deprived, for the poverty stricken in our society... we now have in this country eight million low paid workers, by any definition low paid, taking home not just 60 or 70 but some of the home workers in some of the other industries 50, 55, for full working weeks. So we want to remind people that you cannot go on in a country such as ours, which is one of the twenty richest nations on earth, exploiting people. That is what has happened all these years. That is what has happened particularly these last eight years... Mrs. Thatcher and her Britain, a country divided, north and south, rich and poor, those people in work and those out; part-time, temporary jobs on the one hand, secure and well-paid ones on the other; the land of the dispossessed, one in nine of the adult population out of work, deserted, discarded, not wanted in Thatcher's new society. ❞
Rodney Bickerstaffe at the National Conference of NUPE, May 1987

NUPE members in Hackney.
SUNIL GUPTA

1983, the Labour Party adopted as policy 'the introduction of a statutory minimum wage, with a minimum wage target set at no less than two thirds of national average earnings.' Two years later, the Party Conference supported the policy by the two thirds majority necessary to make it the official policy of the Labour Party. This was followed, in 1986, by TUC endorsement of NUPE's call for a statutory minimum wage.

For years before, both the TUC and Labour Party had given support to motions opposing low pay and had even laid down targets for minimum earnings, but they always drew back from commitment to a statutory minimum wage. Other unions feared that the statutory minimum would quickly become a maximum, that defensible wage differentials would be eroded, that the policy would usher in another period of government-imposed incomes policy and that it would interfere with free collective bargain-

❛ The Government are not only trying to starve our public services of funds. They are also attempting to destroy local democracy by the use of the financial straitjacket into which they are trying to put local authorities...

The Government would like to pretend that the public services are merely parasites on the nation's private manufacturing lifeblood, that they are staffed only by bureaucrats, and bloated bureaucrats at that, living comfortably off the pickings from the national purse. They should try telling that to some of the members of my own union, who feed the children at school, who care for the sick, and look after the elderly, whose dedication is rewarded by pay packets so light that when put on the scales they would scarce outbalance a feather. ❜

Alan Fisher, at the TUC Conference September 1981

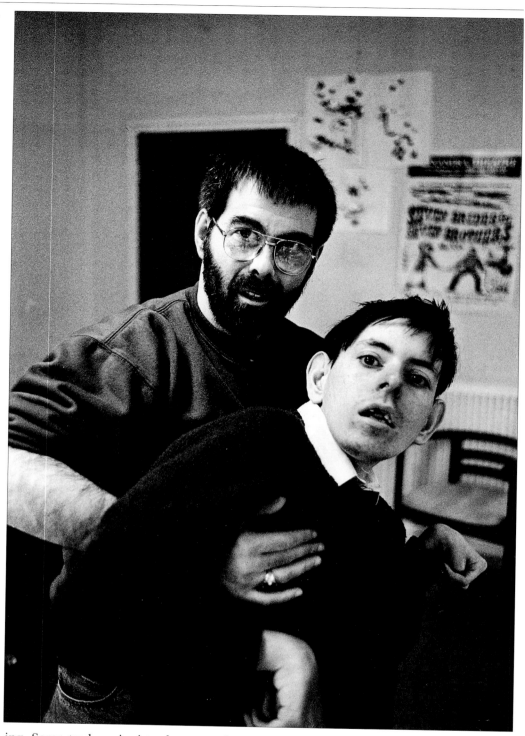

ing. Some trade unionists also went along with those critics from outside the movement who argued that a statutory minimum wage would cause unacceptable levels of inflation, ruin many businesses and put workers on the dole.

However, the experience of a massive increase in the number of workers on low pay under the Tories, the sheer lack of progress in eliminating low wages through collective bargaining, the alarming rise in poverty, and the small prospect of the Tory government introducing radical redistributive tax policies,

combined to eventually force other unions and the TUC to come round to NUPE's position. This was helped by the union's own vigorous campaigns and advocacy. It continued to support and be supported by the Low Pay Unit and Rodney Bickerstaffe was instrumental in establishing the Low Pay Forum, a network of trade unionists, politicians and academics working jointly to make the case for low paid workers and their need for a national minimum wage.

In 1985, NUPE's Executive Council launched its major strategy document, *End*

Democracy Day demonstration,
March 1984.

ANDREW WAIRD / REPORT

Poverty Pay, setting out the long history of the union's campaign against low pay and documenting the continuing problems of low wages in the public services and other industries. It provided a sharp critique of Tory government policies to impose cash limits upon the public sector, extend the scope of privatisation, and abolish existing protection for wages and employment. The document set out NUPE's case for the introduction of a national minimum wage, backed up by the law. It also provided answers to those with anxieties and reservations about the policy.

But, important though these reservations were, requiring proper reassurance and repudiation before wider support could be won, NUPE's new General Secretary saw the low pay issue as part of a more fundamental battle against poverty and inequality in our society. As he declared at the 1984 NUPE National Conference:

> We have said it for years in NUPE, our economy is built on a principle that there is one law for them and another one for us. It is a nation of the rich and the poor. It is a nation that has been built by this government to be a two-tier

nation. We in NUPE do not want any part of those sophisticates who talk about these clever analyses of society and of the economy. We know what it is about. It is simply about the haves, and have-nots, and our members and our families and the people we represent are all in that second section; the have-nots. We have never had it.

The brilliant and often witty oratory of the man destined to be NUPE's last General Secretary was soon to become a main feature of the annual TUC Congress and Labour Party Conference and of trade union platforms across the country. Imbued with his own powerful sense of ethical socialism, Bickerstaffe's persistent advocacy on behalf of low-paid workers was one of the outstanding features of NUPE's history throughout the Thatcher years. This was coupled with his deep hostility to greed, exploitation and selfish individualism. His determination was always to oppose policies which destroyed public services, sacrificed jobs and thus further increased poverty and inequality.

Despite the best efforts of the union, when the latest figures from the New Earnings Sur-

The Thatcher years and after **117**

Birmingham City Council Public Services Festival, 1986.

ROY PETERS PHOTOGRAPHY

vey were published in late 1992, they still made depressing reading. Average wages for full-time ancillary workers in the NHS were still only 70 per cent of those for all workers. Two thirds of male ancillaries and more than four out of five of their female colleagues received less than two hundred pounds gross weekly, which itself was only 59 per cent of average earnings in 1992. The position was not much better for full-time local authority manual workers, where almost 40 per cent of men and three quarters of the women earned less than two hundred pounds gross per week. Part-timers were even worse off. As inequality was sharply increased, the Low Pay Unit's review of Mrs Thatcher's first ten years accu-

rately summed up the consequences of deliberate government policy to redistribute income from the low paid to the rich and super-rich. In a pamphlet with the accurate title, *The Poor Decade*, they concluded:

> The 1980s have been a decade of despair for
> the low paid and their families. Increasing
> numbers have found themselves consigned to
> poverty wages, and many of those who were
> already amongst the poor have seen their
> relative earnings slip still further behind those
> of the rest of the workforce.

DEFENDING THE PUBLIC SERVICES
Alongside the battle for low paid workers,

❛ We do not accept their interpretation about what the miners' dispute is all about. We know what it is about. They have told us often enough. It is about jobs. It is about communities. They are our people, our fathers, brothers, nephews, uncles, they are our people.

The miners' fight is the fight of every man and woman in this country. Everyone of them. The economy is the people and if the people are not working, and are not allowed to work, then the economy cannot work. ❜

Rodney Bickerstaffe in support of the miners, National Conference, May 1984

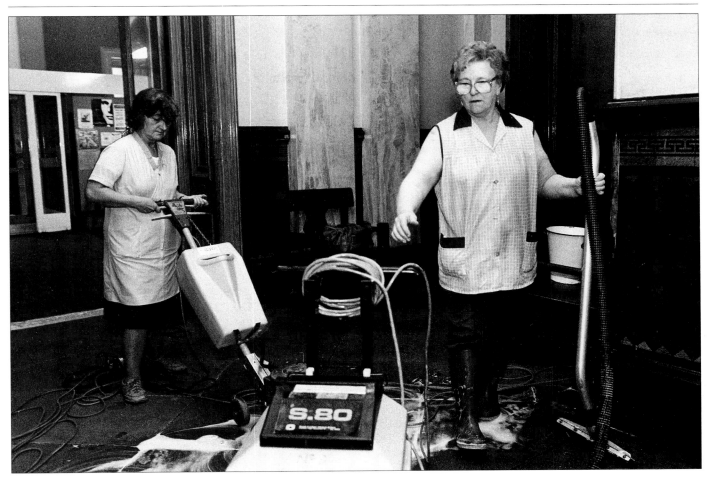

NUPE's biggest fight from 1979 onwards was in defence of the public services themselves. Before they even came to power, the Conservative Party under Mrs Thatcher had made clear their objectives of 'rolling back' the state. From a Tory point of view, public services were inefficient, over-staffed, lacking in choice and, above all, not sufficiently exposed to what the Conservatives saw as the beneficial effects of competition in the marketplace. Workers in the public sector, they argued, including those in management, were artificially insulated from the risks and opportunities experienced by their counterparts in privately-owned industry. In such circumstances, it was hardly surprising, said Thatcher and her strategic advisers, that the public sector was spendthrift and out of control. A main target was provided by local authorities, especially where their elected members offered some opposition to the blitzkrieg of Tory economic and social policy.

Cleaning workers, Liverpool Municipal Offices, 1983.

DENIS DORAN

❛ Ten years ago my predecessor stood here and said, 'I'm worried about what's going to happen, about what this Government is going to do.' Mrs. Thatcher had been in power just 16 days. 'It is quite clear to me', Alan said, 'that we are going to have very real difficulties.' It was a bit of an understatement, but how right he was. Cuts in public spending, promised by the incoming Tory Government, hitting not just public sector workers but all workers. He went on to predict that unemployment would rise by well over two million in the next few years. Even more astutely, he said back then that when unemployment rose 'I do not think Mrs. Thatcher is going to do a U-turn', and there has been no U-turn on that. No U-turn from bashing the unions, bashing the unemployed, creating divisions in this so-called United Kingdom. No U-turn from penalising the poor and rewarding the rich, from policies based on greed. ❜

Rodney Bickerstaffe at the National Conference of NUPE, May 1989

Once in office, and with an overall economic policy obsessively driven by monetarist considerations, it was natural that the Thatcher government should target public spending, public provision and the pay and jobs of public sector workers. Within such a strategy, the opportunities for revenge against public sector unions on the one hand, and for facilitating private profits on the other, were a definite added bonus. Thus the Tories embarked on a long-term and radical restructuring of state provision in this country. In a breathtaking programme of privatisation, the Government set about selling and hiving-off major public assets, such as Britoil, British Telecom, British Gas, British Airways, local authority housing, and the supply and generation of electricity. Altogether, the sale of public assets realised for the Conservative governments just under 26 billion, and even then critics from the Right argued that the sales could have produced more than 4.6 billion more. As it was, underwriters were able to make 10.6 per cent profit on their commitment. For the Tories, the sales constituted an enormous windfall, to be used to fund tax cuts and to disguise the serious state of the British economy.

The caring union.
A. NICOLA

Where outright sale or dismemberment was not immediately available, so-called 'de-regulation' was introduced, as in the case of bus transport, and scope was given for private contractors to bid to take over tasks previous-ly performed by directly employed staff. Schools were first given their own budgets, in the development of local management, and then encouraged to break away entirely from local authority control, lured partly by the promise of additional funding, to become 'grant-maintained'. Long before detailed plans were brought forward, often for only cursory and inadequate scrutiny by Parlia-ment, plans were announced or strongly hinted at for privatisation measures of one kind or another in water, railways and the mines.

Although she did little to disguise her hos-tility to local government, especially when under Labour control, Mrs Thatcher sought to reassure the nation that the National Health Service was 'safe' in her hands. Al-though few believed her and support for the health service remained high, this did not prevent the widespread introduction of pri-vate contractors, seeking especially to replace the jobs done by the direct employment of ancillary workers in the health service, just as they were those of manual workers in local government.

In 1983, health authorities were instructed to put the work of catering, domestic and laundry staff out to competitive tender. Sepa-rate Local Government Acts in 1980 and 1988 obliged councils to seek tenders for building, highways, refuse collection, clean-ing, catering, vehicle and ground mainte-nance and the management of sports and leisure facilities. Although council depart-ments could compete for the contracts them-selves, they could only do so after meeting stringent conditions. In practice, where con-tracts were won 'in-house', this frequently en-tailed a combination of job losses, reductions in hours, a reorganisation of working prac-tices, loss of bonuses and, frequently, a re-duction in the extent and quality of the ser-vice.

NUPE was quick to point out the true mo-tives behind the Government's policies in the speeches of its representatives and in confer-

The 1980s saw significant campaigns in support of the school meals service.
SHEILA GRAY

ence motions. They were, said the union in its many publications, a deliberate and direct attack on local democracy. Compulsory competitive tendering, argued the union, was unlikely, in the end, to provide the savings in costs and other improvements promised. Instead they would lower the living standards of workers, bring damage to local economies, reduce standards of service provision, create industrial relations problems and substitute the pursuit of private profit for the meeting of social needs.

None of this mattered much to unscrupulous Tory councils, eager to reduce council spending and sacrifice local services for the benefit of political gain. Some Conservative-controlled councils set about the task of dismantling their own provision of services with relish: Wandsworth, Southend, Basingstoke, and Gloucester were the locations of only some of the most notorious moves to dump direct employment, and they produced from NUPE notable mobilisations of resistance. Some health authorities also eagerly went out to tender, provoking bitter, long drawn-out strikes, some of them lasting over a year, in

Barking, Essex, Newcastle and at Addenbrookes Hospital in Cambridge, amongst others. Jobs were lost, pay reduced, hours cut back and holiday entitlement slashed by contractors. In-house bids were forced to compete with the determination of large multinational companies and their subsidiaries, bent on winning contracts principally by attacking staff pay and conditions.

The challenge of all of this to NUPE was enormous. Low-paid workers, many already struggling to make ends meet, were in the front line of attack. NUPE's campaign over the years had been for a national minimum wage, but now its members faced the prospect of even lower standards of pay and conditions. The Government's policies also threatened NUPE's political support for the public provision of local services. Its whole growth and very being had been coincidental with the successful establishment of local democracy, the welfare state and free health care at the point of delivery. Even the School Meals Service, which had done so much to improve standards of nutrition for children, was at risk.

County roadmen in 1983.
VIEWPOINT

Along with other public service unions, it was necessary for NUPE to act, quickly and with some purpose. As well as campaigning vigorously for support at the TUC and in the Labour Party, the union mounted a huge publicity campaign in defence of public services It drew attention to the high incidence of private contractors' failures and supported local initiatives to improve service quality, involve workers and users more and expand service provision shop stewards and other branch officials were trained and encouraged to get involved in discussions to win tenders in-house and fight to maintain jobs and conditions where outside contractors were introduced. When Tory proposals to allow hospi-

❛ The sub-title of the Queen's Speech this year might well have been 'How we plan to destroy local government'. There are some in the Tory Party who are honest enough to say what they think. They do not like local government because it gives people a chance to vote for the services they need and to have some control over them, but we know what kind of local government the Government wants. It is local government in which the councillors meet once a year to hand out the contracts, and the rest is done by private profiteers...

There is a lot of jargon talked about privatising services. There are specifications and in-house tenders, and rates of return on capital, but... what it all boils down to at the end of the day is brutally simple. The message to a million council workers is clear: 'Take a pay cut or get the sack', and anyone who thinks that is scaremongering should listen to what the audit commissioners said. One in three council jobs will go in the next five years. Never mind if you have got 20 or 30 years loyal service behind you, never mind if you have got training and experience, never mind if you are dedicated to working in the caring services...

The threat to local government is not just about jobs and pay, important though that is for the workers whose jobs are at risk. It is about standards and about quality. It is about the principles of public service against the pursuit of private profit. It is about democracy: local communities deciding on the local services that they want. That is why we all have to take a stand, not just the local government unions but all of us. ❜
Rodney Bickerstaffe at the TUC Conference 1987

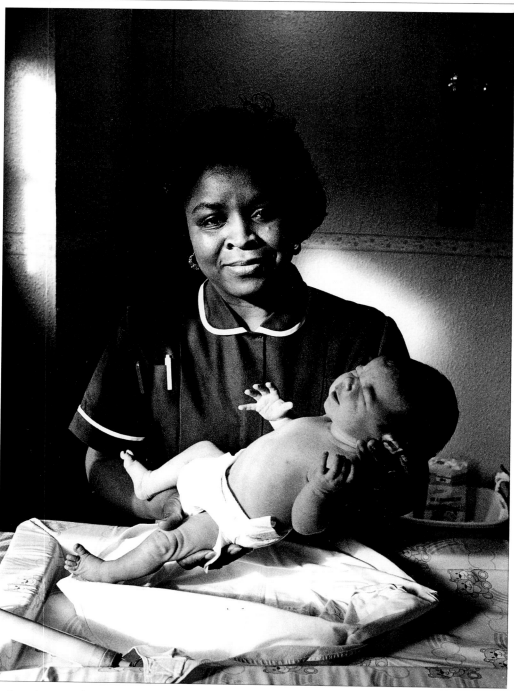

tals to 'opt out' of health authority were announced, NUPE accused the Government of wanting to dismantle the National Health Service.

NUPE also helped to found, and then fund, both the Local Government Information Unit (LGIU) and the joint-union Public Services Privatisation Research Unit (PSPRU), which was housed in NUPE's purpose-built headquarters in Woolwich, where the union had moved from Lewisham. Excellent advice on privatisation and tendering was provided to local authorities and trade unions by the LGIU. The PSPRU, supported by COHSE, NALGO, NIPSA, NUCPS, NUPE

and TGWU, established a detailed data-base about contracts and contract failures, hours of work, pay, conditions and the ownership of private contractor companies. This was part of a wider move towards trade union unity, as unions in the public services joined forces to defend their members and the services themselves. NUPE had already formed a joint Liaison Committee with NALGO, in 1976, with whom it launched a defence of local government in 1980. Similar arrangements for a joint liaison committee with COHSE at national level were in the Executive Council's Report to NUPE's Conference in 1984.

In a major review of privatisation, *Disaster for Quality*, published in March 1992, the PSPRU documented that private contractors held a quarter of the more than 2000 contracts put out to tender. In 28 per cent of them, there had been problems, by contrast with only 6 per cent of those won in-house. Ten per cent of private contracts from local authorities had been terminated. In the NHS, a quarter of all contracts had gone to private firms as had almost one third of cleaning contracts. Here again, there had been extensive problems with private contractors, and more and more contracts were being awarded or returned to in-house bids, after the initial enthusiasm for the use of out-side contractors had failed to deliver adequate services.

But the costs to NUPE's low-paid members had been dear. According to information collected by the Unit, 111,000 jobs had been lost in the NHS in England and Wales between 1983 and 1991, of which 90,000 were held by women. Between 1988 and 1991, manual workers in British councils had been cut by more than 114,000. In the NHS, contractors typically had worse conditions for hours worked, pay, sick pay, pensions and maternity provision. The Unit estimated that the loss of pay and conditions to local government workers was worth 125 million per year. Private contractors were rife, too, in the priva-

Nottingham health workers during a NHS day of action, February 1988.

MARTIN JENKINSON

6 Added up, the NHS White Paper amounts to a blueprint for a two-tier health system, with the NHS starved of funding, providing emergency services and basic care, while the state subsidies help the better off to buy care from the private sector, encouraging private medicine to flourish. And what about our people, the women, the main users of the health service, children, the elderly and carers for the elderly, mostly women, and the poorest? They will be hard hit too. 9

Rodney Bickerstaffe at the National Conference of NUPE, May 1989

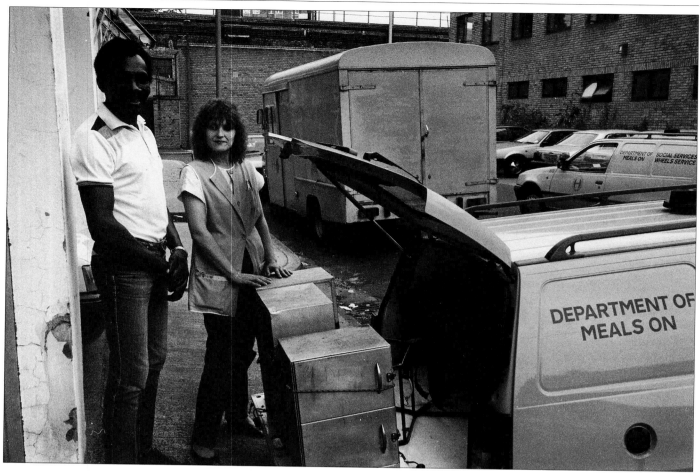

NUPE members, Hackney
Meals on Wheels.
SUNIL GUPTA

tised water industry and NUPE's members in Further and Higher Education feared for their jobs and conditions of service, as the Government removed first polytechnics and then further education from the control of local authorities. Recognition for manual and white-collar workers' trade unionism in the universities, especially some of the older ones, had been hard won and the achievement of a 'spheres of influence' agreement by NUPE and other unions in the late 1970s had represented a great step forward for non-teaching staff working in the universities.

DISPUTES AND TRADE UNION SOLIDARITY
By the time John Major had taken over as leader of the Tories, and won for them their fourth successive victory in a general election, one of the Government's proudest boasts was the big reduction they had secured in strikes and other industrial disputes. It was not without some justification. Nor had such a dramatic decline been effected without fierce trade union resistance. The miners had fought a year-long battle against pit closures and the seafarers and newspaper printers had fallen foul of employer intransigence

and the juridical application of the Thatcher anti-union laws. In all three cases, NUPE had been one of those unions to offer solidarity and support, including the provision of financial aid. During the epic struggle of the miners, NUPE had donated £100,000 in support and had loaned the NUM a further £340,000. But during this period NUPE was also caught up in its own disputes to save jobs and services and in support of claims for pay increases, and it did not always receive the degree of wider trade union support that it would have liked.

The first of these was the eight-month long NHS dispute in 1982. It was a baptism of fire for NUPE's new leadership, and its highlights included a huge rally in London on 22 September, attended by an estimated 120,000 marchers, the largest week-day demonstration in the capital since the Second World War. Altogether, more than 800,000 working days were lost in the health service strike action, in what was by far the longest industrial dispute faced by the first Thatcher government. But, it was not just the duration of the dispute which was significant, nor even NUPE members' involvement in it. The Gov-

ernment found itself on the defensive as, for the first time in this period, it discovered that the public popularity of the NHS afforded the service some degree of protection against attack. A public opinion poll taken at the end of 1981 had indicated that more than seven out of ten of those interviewed thought that the National Health Service represented good value for the taxpayer, and nine out of ten respondents said they received good service from their hospital.

Yet again, it was government pay policy which had triggered the action. It had set 'guidelines' for an overall limit of 4 per cent on pay rises in the public sector: the unions' pay claim was for a 12 per cent increase. This would simply have preserved the real value of NHS pay for ancillary workers, nursing auxiliaries and maintenance staff. Nurses' wages had fallen back since the Halsbury award and between 1975 and 1982, the real value of their pay had declined by 3.5 per cent whilst average real earnings had increased by almost the same amount. Average earnings of female ancillary workers in 1981 stood at only 54 per cent of average earnings across the country. In early May, NUPE announced the

results of its branch ballot on the 4 per cent offer, with 191,000 rejecting the offer and only 1200 prepared to accept it. Later that same month, the union's National Conference voted for strike action and in early June even the RCN rejected the offer by a majority of two to one.

A key feature of the dispute, and one which was to become of increasing significance throughout the decade, was the eventual unity attained between the thirteen different TUC unions involved. After a start to the dispute which was somewhat bedevilled by differences between the unions, the TUC Health Services Committee became closely involved from early June. It called for a three-day stoppage in July. Miners in Yorkshire, Derbyshire, Nottingham, the Midlands, South Wales and Scotland all took industrial action in support of the health workers. On the day of the London demonstration, rallies were held all over the country, with over 50,000 reported to have taken part in various Scottish cities, 20,000 in Liverpool and 10,000 in Sheffield.

However, this was not the government of Edward Heath. It stood firm after failing to

At the end of the march, Birmingham 1988.
ROY PETERS PHOTOGRAPHY

Parkview vehicle maintenance department, Haringey, 1988.
PHILIP WOLMUTH

divide the unions and different occupational groups with varying offers. After the longest-ever dispute in the NHS, NUPE's health service members and its Executive Council were forced to accept a deal agreed by all the TUC health unions just before Christmas. In retrospect, it was realised that the only way the health workers could have won outright was by all-out support action in all industries and services and by the complete withdrawal of services, something the Executive was unwilling to recommend and NUPE's members would have been quite unwilling to implement.

Even so, industrial action was not yet over for NUPE members. Before the dispute in the NHS was over, the union's water industry members had balloted in favour of industrial action to support their claim for parity with workers in gas and electricity supply. The Government responded by announcing the disbanding of the National Water Council which raised the threat of an end to national pay agreements. If anything, this spurred the members into even more determined action and, at the end of five weeks of solid, all-out

strike action, they won a pay increase of 11.5 per cent.

Of all NUPE's disputes in this period, it was undoubtedly that of the ambulance staffs in the winter of 1988-89 which left the biggest impression. This was not because of the numbers involved, nor because of the eventual size of the pay settlement they achieved after a six-month campaign of strike action, in support of a claim for a pay formula like that won by the firefighters in their 1977 dispute with the Labour Government. Nor was it even because of the overwhelming support the ambulance crews received from the general public, including the donation of large amounts of cash. The chief reason why the dispute had such an impact was that the handling of it, by the officers and members of all the unions involved, was exemplary.

With Roger Poole, NUPE's National Secretary, acting as spokesperson for ambulance staffs in COHSE, NALGO, the TGWU and GMB, as well as for his own members in NUPE, the unions handed out a public relations good hiding to one of the Tory heavyweights, Ken Clarke. Their skilful use of the media was outstanding, as was their refusal to be provoked by Clarke's general bumptiousness and his contemptuous dismissal of ambulance crews as 'taxi-drivers'. Above all, the ambulance dispute demonstrated the value of unity and common purpose amongst public service workers. Experience of successful united action in the ambulance dispute was to make an important contribution to the negotiations for a new public service union, which had begun between NUPE and NALGO in 1988 and which COHSE joined in 1989, just as the action in the ambulance service was beginning.

THE LABOUR PARTY

From the very formation of the Labour Representation Committee and subsequently of the Labour Party itself, NUPE had been a strong supporter and affiliate. In 1981, shortly before his retirement, Bernard Dix became the first officer of the union to be elected to the Party's National Executive. He was followed by Tom Sawyer, who eventually became one of the most influential national figures in the Party, advocating and helping to carry through the Party's extensive Policy Review, implemented after Labour's third successive general election defeat in 1987. As NUPE moved closer to centre stage in the affairs of the Party, this was yet a further signal of its growing recognition in the otherwise bleak years of Conservative rule from 1979 onwards.

Following the enactment of the 1984 Trade Union Act, NUPE and other unions affiliated to the Labour Party were obliged to ballot their members on their willingness for the union to maintain the political funds, which trade unions had been able to establish since before the First World War. The Government's proposals caused outrage and

Mrs Thatcher was accused, not only of attacking unions' right to spend their own funds as they saw fit, but also of attempting to destroy the Labour Party itself. As Tom Sawyer eloquently put it, to NUPE's 1984 National Conference, the proposal to impose political fund ballots on the unions had to be seen in the wider context of Tory policy:

> The Tories would love to see the trade union links with the Labour Party broken. They would love to see millions of working people separate from the Labour Party, negotiating no-strike agreements with employers, selling flags outside hospitals instead of fighting for public services and fighting to end cuts and privatisation. It would be right in line with their policy of eliminating all centres of opposition, weakening the trade unions through pay cuts, unemployment and privatisation, isolating the unemployed through divisions and separation, and silencing people like the Greenham Common women by preventing their case from being heard by the British public… Of course, they do not just want to break the trade union links with the Labour Party, they want to destroy the party of the working class itself.

The next year, in one of the wittiest and most effective speeches ever heard at a NUPE conference, Sawyer appeared with a shopping bag, to illustrate the indirect contributions to Tory Party funds derived from the profits on everyday household products. Once again, he pointed out the clear aims of the Government's latest anti-union legislation: 'when the Tories introduced this legislation, they had one aim in mind: to destroy the links between the trade unions and the Labour Party'. The Deputy General Secretary exhorted the union's members to make their voice heard,

6 When it comes to hypocrisy, the real people, the people who win the gold medals and the cups for outstanding performances in hypocrisy, are the Tory Party who introduce legislation on trade union political funds yet who at the same time expect hundreds, thousands, millions of pounds of our money, through the goods we buy from the companies which donate to Tory Party funds. They are the real hypocrites. 9
Tom Sawyer at the National Conference of NUPE, May 1985

and deliver an overwhelming vote in favour of maintaining links with the Party:

'Say yes to a political voice', the slogan on our platform for this conference, is a message of major importance. It's not just another ballot, not just another test of members' opinion but a new and important opportunity to argue, mobilise, organise and win support for a renewal of our political commitment to the union and our support for the Labour Party.

Following an extensive campaign, itself part of a wider national trade union effort superbly orchestrated by the all-union Trade Union Co-ordinating Committee, and after making widespread use of the union's network of union stewards to canvass NUPE members, almost 400,000 took part in the union's ballot, a turn-out of 60 per cent. When the result was announced in January 1986, it revealed that 84 per cent of those voting had voted in favour of retaining the links. However, once more, NUPE's hopes for a Labour victory at the polls in 1987 were to be gravely disappointed, as they had been in 1983 and were to be, yet again, in 1992.

WORKING FOR EQUALITY

From their very beginnings, partially reflecting a wider sexual division of labour in British society, the public services in Britain had provided paid employment to women workers. In the National Health Service, they had always constituted a majority. Little of this was reflected in the organisation and structure of British unions. By the time of the 'Warwick' reforms of NUPE, the union could already count more than 300,000 female members amongst its ranks, but there was not a single woman member on its Executive Council. Alongside local initiatives to give a greater say to the union's women members, the introduction of reserved seats for women in 1975 had begun to provide greater opportunities for women to increase their participation in the centres of power in NUPE, and thus to help to shape the union's agenda. In 1982, a third of NUPE's Executive was composed of women, but an Executive Council review of progress with the union's reorganisation felt that 'the stage has not been reached when the reserved seats can be abolished.' In the meantime, female members of the union had also increasingly become stewards, branch and district secretaries and conference delegates. By the end of 1983 no less than 44 per cent of NUPE stewards were women.

In 1982 Olwen Davies, a hospital worker

❝ We played a part in that policy review because we believed that, after three election defeats, it was important that Labour listened and learned from the people. It was time that we fought in NUPE for Labour to broaden its appeal, time for Labour to start winning general elections again and time for Labour to start speaking out for those in work as well as for those out of work, time for Labour to speak for those who do not depend on welfare as well as for those who do, for those who expect to enjoy a relatively high standard of living as well as for those whose living standards can only improve under Labour.

That is what the policy review has been about, and that is why it has been important. It is not about throwing out Labour principles, it is about putting them into practice, about making the policies of the Labour Party relevant to the needs of the working people in the 1990s. It means talking to the people that we need to win, people who do not want to know how bad it was before Labour took office in 1945 but about how good it will be when Labour has been in power for four years in 1995, that is what the people want to know about. They do not want slogans or long lists of resolutions that can never be implemented because you are never in power to do it. They do not want resolutions, they want reasoned, sensible arguments that they can understand. Most of all, they do not want to be told what is best for them, because that is the way of Mrs. Thatcher, and people have had enough of being lectured by politicians. ❞

Tom Sawyer at the National Conference of NUPE, May 1989

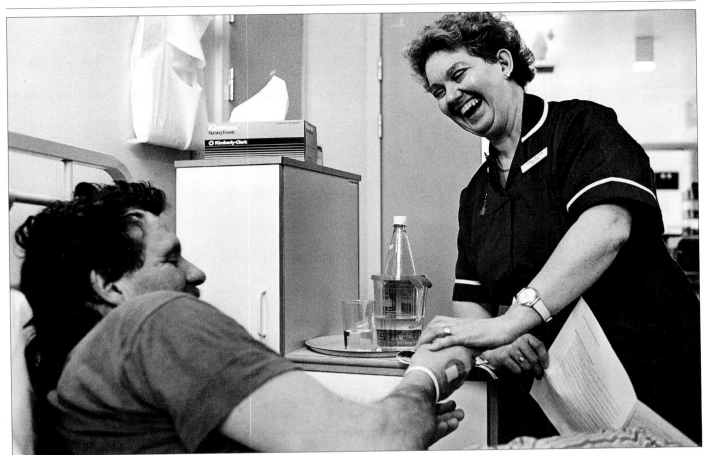

Ward sister in Stoke-on-Trent.
ROY PETERS PHOTOGRAPHY

from South Wales, became NUPE's first female President. She was followed over the next ten years by a further six women Presidents. Women members also began to play a larger role on NUPE's behalf in the wider labour movement. In 1983, Lil Stevens, a school meals supervisor from Birmingham and the union's second woman President, became the first female British trade unionist for thirty years to be elected to a 'general' seat of the General Council of the TUC. In 1981 Lil had received the TUC Women's Gold Badge, an honour which was to be won by another NUPE woman President, Ina Love, six years later in 1987.

NUPE's women members also figured strongly in the union's defence of the public services in the 1970s and 1980s, especially the NHS and the school meals service. But their position in the union and their influence upon the union's agenda still did not adequately reflect their numbers in the union and their key role in the provision of public services. Accordingly, in 1982 NUPE established a Women's Working Party, which produced a far-reaching report in January 1984. In addition to confirming its support for the appointment of NUPE's first Women's Offi-

cer, the Working Party argued that the union should 'continue its programme of positive action'. The aim should be to get more women involved, and to achieve proper levels of representation of women generally, and of occupations such as school meals and nursing in which women were the majority.

At the time of the Working Party's report, there were still only nine women on NUPE's four National Committees, compared with forty-two men. A chief aim of NUPE's next steps in advancing the position of its women members should be to get 'the particular perspective of women into the forefront of our thinking and the mainstream of the union's work.' The Report went on to make specific recommendations on Branch organisation, including the timing of, location and access to meetings and the provision of child care support. More workplace and sectional meetings would help women's participation, as would less formality in the conduct of union meetings. Branches should elect Women's Liaison Officers and establish Equality Committees.

At Divisional level, the Working Party advised that the role of Women's Advisory Committees should be strengthened, and the

NUPE clerical members, 1988.

SUNIL GUPTA

secretary should be a woman full-time officer or member. At national level, a National Women's Committee should be established, reporting directly to the Executive Council and serviced by the union's Women's Officer. Finally, greater attention should be given to the recruitment of women members and to the provision of union education facilities for women, 'which offer an informal, supportive environment and are run by women tutors.' The inaugural meeting of the union's Women's National Advisory Committee was held in January 1985.

When the union's major consultative report on women was produced in 1989, *Women in NUPE: the Agenda for the 90s*, it was able to report that almost 50 per cent of the Executive were women. The union's branch survey, conducted in 1988, had demonstrated that action had been taken in a third of the branches to secure time off for union meetings and to make them more interesting. A sixth of the branches responding were providing for childcare and most were avoiding meetings in pubs. However, most had neither a Women's Liaison Officer nor an

132   *A Century of Service*

Equality Committee and many continued to meet mostly in the evenings. The document advocated a 'higher negotiating profile' for equal rights for women and for more union initiatives for black women members facing problems of racial discrimination and racism.

The issue of NUPE's black members had also come onto the union's agenda in the 1980s. After two years' work, the union's Race Equality Working Party produced a report underlining the important role of black workers in the provision of Britain's public services and the problems they faced of racial hostility and under-representation in trade union and other power structures. A mere glance at the pages of the union's journals in the 1980s was sufficient to underline the valuable role played by NUPE's black members, especially women, in the union's campaigns. Their active participation in NUPE's rallies, demonstrations and disputes in defence of the National Health Service was not, however, mirrored in their involvement in the union's representative and decision-making structures.

After detailing several initiatives required to combat racism at work and in the community, the Working Party also advocated action at all levels in the union itself. Its proposals ranged from the workplace and Branch through to the establishment of Divisional and National Race Advisory Committees. Two new union rules were proposed and subsequently approved, to include a positive commitment to racial equality, combat racism and make racist behaviour a matter for union discipline. Recognising that combatting racism was not just a question of union rules and discipline, the NUPE *Journal* also carried several major features on race and racism. For their part, the union's negotiators made increased efforts to point out instances of racial discrimination in appointments and grading systems.

RESPONSIVE TRADE UNIONISM

From 1979 onwards, during fourteen years of unrelenting attack and huge membership decline, the British trade union movement was obliged to take a careful look at itself. This meant changing its systems of election and decision-making, with increasing reliance on individual ballots. The unions were required to examine more carefully the composition of their membership and the extent to which members were being adequately represented; new membership services were demanded and provided. Trade union methods, tactics and organisation all underwent changes of approach and emphasis and throughout

❛ But it is not only the Tories who think that democracy starts and ends at the ballot box. We have got some in our own ranks, the same people who want to sign no-strike deals or no-disruption agreements. It is the same people who want non-political trade unionism. They call themselves 'new realists'…

We do not want new realism. We call it 'old dealism'. We do not want to do deals behind closed doors with any government, whether Labour or Conservative. We want strong, independent trade unions with organised, educated members, ready to fight for their rights at work with industrial action where necessary.

Yes, we want to be professional. We want to be more efficient. We want to give good service to our fellow members, but not at the price of democracy…

What we want is a tough, tested, reliable, old-fashioned approach. It is called 'trade union solidarity', in case anyone has forgotten what its name is. We have got to face today's problems with that kind of industrial approach which, of course, will have an important political dimension, which includes supporting the Labour Party, but which does not end there, because our political approach must be bigger than willing support for the Labour Party, it must talk about uniting all working people, including the unemployed and the women at Greenham Common and anyone who needs the strength of the working class, to fight together to build democratic socialism. ❜

Tom Sawyer at the National Conference of NUPE, May 1984

Pensive moment. A Walsall health worker pauses to reflect on what the future may bring.
ROY PETERS PHOTOGRAPHY

> **6** NUPE is Britain's leading women's union. We lead in membership and we lead on policies, yet inequality still persists against women and against black people both outside NUPE and, unfortunately, within NUPE itself...NUPE women can be proud of their achievements in this union, but there is a lot more to be done. We are still under-represented throughout the union's structures, and equality policies need more translating into action. **9**

Daphne Bullock, Executive Council member, NUPE's centenary conference, 1989

the movement, as in NUPE, voices were increasingly raised inside the unions by women, by black members, by those with disabilities and by lesbians and gay men. Union attitudes to the European Community were sharply revised and new alliances were formed, both with fellow trade unions and with organisations representing other groups and campaigning on behalf of other issues.

In these circumstances, some critics argued that British trade unions were already on a downward spiral, closely following the path taken by organised labour in the USA. Others, perhaps meaning to be more optimistic, called for a radical trade union adjustment to a new era of resurgent capitalism and the death of Soviet-inspired communism and socialism. They called for acceptance of the new political realities of individualism and of Conservative rule. They concluded that this meant an accommodation with the Tories, and acceptance of the bulk of Conservative trade union reforms. Some went as far as advocating putting some distance between the unions and the Labour Party. Initially dubbed the 'new realists', advocates of this approach were later to call themselves 'modernisers' whilst their opponents were referred to as the 'traditionalists'.

NUPE's approach was to reject the new realism and to advocate instead the development of a more responsive style of trade unionism. In addition to giving increased attention to equality issues in the union, this meant placing the union's members more firmly at the centre of initiatives. The union's publications began to give greater emphasis to the working lives and experiences of its members and these became a regular feature of the union's *Journal*. Union publications were directed towards the particular concerns of members, such as home helps, school meals staff and workers in the volun-

tary sector. A detailed report was issued calling for a *Fair Deal for Part-time Workers*, following the union's successful motion on the same topic at the 1985 TUC.

Despite the success of the reforms which had followed the Warwick Report, much remained to be done to involve the union's members more directly in its democracy and organisation. Pressures of work, caring and other domestic responsibilities, and the wide dispersal of workplaces, still meant that the formal machinery of the union was somewhat remote to many. Partly to combat this, new forms of communication were implemented, including re-modelling NUPE's members' journal, first to incorporate colour (in 1983) and later, to assume a magazine-style format. In 1992, the union introduced direct mailing of the journal to members' homes for the first time. These developments proved popular with NUPE's membership and the *NUPE Journal* won several competitions and awards for its journalism, design and presentation. Similarly, along with many other unions, NUPE introduced greater use of membership surveys and polling, to supplement the union's established methods of consultation and communication.

As a contribution to improving services to members, in the late 1980s the union's education service successfully developed an exciting and successful scheme of 'open learning', with its popular Return to Learn programme, first piloted with the WEA in the West Midlands. This complemented the union's earlier initiative, which began in London, in supporting Workbase, an innovative workplace educational scheme for literacy and numeracy. In the late 1980s, the union also implemented an extremely successful programme of systematically recruiting and training 'Trainee' Area Officers, drawn largely from the ranks of NUPE's own members

Local authority grave-digger, 1986.

ROY PETERS PHOTOGRAPHY

and comprised of a majority of women. In the Labour Party's review of its links with the trade unions in 1992-93, NUPE's voice was one of the most powerful in favour of maintaining and even strengthening the links. However, the union was also keen to provided a greater involvement in the Party for its 500,000 payers of the union's political levy.

Part of NUPE's increased emphasis on trade union responsiveness was its support for closer links between the providers of public services, the union's own members, and the users of them amongst the wider general public. Almost twenty years of restrictions on public expenditure, Tory attacks on the very idea of public provision and threats to NUPE members' jobs from private contactors, had all brought home to NUPE its own interests in paying closer attention than hitherto to improving the quality and accessibility of those same services. Negotiating for proper vocational training for NUPE members, including where appropriate providing recognised certification of skills, was added to the bargaining agenda. In defending the jobs of it members and seeking to improve the quality of provision, the union hoped also to continue its defence of the public services themselves.

TOWARDS A NEW UNION

In 1988, just one year before celebrating the union's centenary, the NUPE National Conference took what was to be its most important decision since the foundation of the union. A motion was approved instructing the Executive Council to carry out a feasibility study into the possibility of forming a single public service union, with NALGO and COHSE in the first instance. This had been a dream and ambition for generations of NUPE members and full-time officials. Industrial unionism had been Jack Wills' specialism, before he joined the Corporation Workers, and advocacy of the same had cost Bryn Roberts dear amongst his fellow General Secretaries at the TUC.

In the changed trade union circumstances of the 1980s and after more than a decade of closer, if sometimes hesitant, joint and supportive action, was the time now propitious for such a move? Admittedly, it had often proved easier for the unions to co-operate na-

tionally than on a local level. The obstacles to merger were formidable.

Whereas both NUPE and COHSE were firmly committed to Labour Party affiliation, NALGO was equally determined to maintain its political independence, even though it had won overwhelming membership support for establishing a political fund, after being challenged in the courts over expenditure. COHSE saw itself as a 'specialist' health service union, needing to compete professionally with bodies such as the RCN. In local government, many NUPE members saw NALGO as the 'bosses union', and some laid part of the blame for the damaging effects of compulsory competitive tendering at the door of NALGO-organised local government officers. Moreover, NALGO had members in gas,

electricity and transport, unlike either NUPE or COHSE. And COHSE's membership was four-fifths female and NUPE's women constituted three-quarters of its members, whereas NALGO was roughly split 50:50 between male and female members.

For its part, NALGO had suffered few of the membership losses experienced by the other two unions, especially NUPE, and, in any case it saw itself as a thriving, well-off and campaigning union. In contrast to COHSE and NUPE especially, NALGO activists and members regarded their own union as more democratic and membership controlled. NUPE's tradition, despite the Warwick reforms, appeared to NALGO, at least, to place heavier reliance on the initiative of paid full-time officials. NALGO's local branches were responsible for collecting members' contributions from employers and they fiercely defended branch autonomy. By contrast, NUPE and COHSE had each developed the central collection of subscriptions.

All of this presented a huge task for those in support of merger. Although the NALGO National Conference had also approved a motion calling for its NEC to produce a report on possible merger and the obstacles to overcome, COHSE's Conference declined to join the talks until the following year, and then only as part of a 'twin-track' approach. Even so, senior representatives of NUPE and NALGO began discussions in the autumn of 1988 and so began a careful, painstaking but, ultimately, fruitful series of negotiations which were to last right up to the decisions of

Some members of the Executive Council and Senior Officers at a meeting, April 1993.

PHILIP WOLMUTH

the three unions' National Conferences in the summer of 1992. Then, all three approved the third joint report of the three Executives containing final proposals for a three-way amalgamation to form a new public services union, to be called UNISON, and to start work in July 1993. Decisions were made to trigger membership ballots in the autumn and to launch campaigns for a vote in favour of merger.

The new union would be made up of almost one and a half million members, two-thirds of whom would be women. It would be based firmly on a commitment to the public provision of services, equal opportunities and recognition of the diversity and variety of it members and potential members. For the first time ever, a British union would provide for the proportional representation of women in its decision-making structures and special provision would be made to ensure fair representation for lower paid workers and those from the smaller and more specialist industrial and occupational groups. Authority and initiative would be devolved to UNISON's thirteen regions and seven powerful Service Groups.

In recognition of the different political traditions of the partner unions, arrangements

were also proposed to maintain two distinct political funds, one providing for Labour Party affiliation and the other to support the continuation of wider and independent political action on behalf of members. Holding it all together, the three unions' proposals in favour of amalgamation included a common commitment to create a new culture peculiar to UNISON and its members, reflecting an agreed code of new union objects, aims and values.

When the results of the membership amalgamation ballot were declared, on 16 December 1992, members of all three unions had overwhelmingly supported the recommendation for merger to form UNISON. Over 90 per cent of those voting in NUPE and COHSE and three quarters in NALGO signalled their approval of the new union. It would be the largest trade union in the United Kingdom and one of the largest in the world. It would bring together workers in a wide range of services and occupations and constitute a powerful voice on behalf of services to the public. Above all, it represented a huge beginning to the magnificent achievement of NUPE's hundred-year dream of unity amongst British public service trade unionists.

General Secretaries and Presidents

1889-93

Official records of NUPE's predecessor unions are not complete and it is therefore not possible to provide a comprehensive list of General Secretaries and Presidents. Where the area of residence is known, it is given, as is the first name by which the individual was/is known in the union.

National Municipal Incorporated Vestry Employees Labour Union

(after 1894 the National Municipal Labour Union)

GENERAL SECRETARIES

1889-1890	William Coote	Camberwell
1891-1894	John Cole	Camberwell
1894-1899	John Fitch	Greenwich
1899	Herbert Day	
1900	George Hibbard	Hackney

PRESIDENTS

1889-1893	Wiliam Coote	Camberwell
1893-1898	J. Harding	Camberwell
1899	F. Francis	St Pancras

London County Council Employees Protection Association

(after 1899 the Municipal Employees Association)

GENERAL SECRETARIES

1894-1896	William Anderson	Bow
1896-1907	Albin Taylor	East Ham

PRESIDENTS

1894	J.S. Thomas	Sutton
1901-1902	T. Durrant	
1903-1904	William Steadman	Mile End
1905-1906	William Steadman (Honorary President)	
1905	W.R. Ives (Chairman of Executive Council)	Poplar ·
1906	Richard Baldwin (Chairman of ExecutiveCouncil)	Leicester

National Union of Corporation Workers

(after 1928 the National Union of Public Employees)

GENERAL SECRETARIES

1907-1925	Albin Taylor	East Ham
1925-1933	Jack Wills	Bermondsey
1934-1962	Bryn Roberts	Abertillery/London
1962-1967	Sydney Hill	Dudley/London
1968-1982	Alan Fisher	Birmingham/London
1982-1993	Rodney Bickerstaffe	South Yorkshire/London

PRESIDENTS

1907-1909	J.F. Hart	Stepney
1909-1912	J.J. W Bradley (Jim)	Bethnal Green
1912-1915	T. McGrath (Tom)	St Marylebone
1915-1917	W. Conquer (Walter)	Tottenham
1917-1918	J. Burgess (Joe)	Bermondsey
1918-1920	W.F. Davies	East Ham
1920-1922	S Smith (Sidney)	Epsom
1922-1923	D.G. Stephen (David)	Edinburgh
1923-1924	J.H. Sharp (Joe)	Hornsey
1924-1925	A. Moss (Alfred)	Dewbury
1925-1926	W. Loveland (William)	Leigh on Sea
1926-1927	J.T. Bailey (John)	Wood Green
1927-1928	I. Stokes (Isaiah)	Bermondsey
1928-1929	W. Stevens (Bill)	London
1929-1930	A.W. Hall (Arthur)	Woolwich
1930-1931	C. Agombar (Charles)	Bethnal Green
1931-1932	H.J. Catchpole (Harry)	Ardsley
1932-1934	W.J. Setchell (Bill)	Bermondsey
1934-1935	R.F. Jones (Dick)	Merthyr
1935-1936	A. Walker (Albert)	East Ham
1936-1937	T.N. Kibble (Tommy)	Hampstead
1937-1939	D.G Stephen (David)	Edinburgh
1939-1940	J.O. Smith (Johnnie)	Bethnal Green
1940-1941	R.D. Whitlam (Bobby)	Bermondsey
1941-1942	H.J. Catchpole (Harry)	Ardsley
1942-1943	W. Stevens (Bill)	London
1943-1944	R.F. Jones (Dick)	Merthyr
1944-1945	J. Carwell (Jack)	Blackpool
1945-1946	A. Tugby (Arthur)	Nottingham
1946-1947	W. Stevens (Bill)	London
1947-1948	W.S. Wigg (Sam)	Norwich
1948-1949	H.J. Catchpole (Harry)	Ardsley
1949-1950	F. McFetters (Frank)	Edinburgh
1950-1951	J. Roper (Jim)	Dudley
1951-1952	F.H. Gould (Frank)	Wallasey
1952-1953	A.F. Jeffreys (Arthur)	Woolwich
1953-1954	W.J. Davies	Harrow
1954-1955	D. Ivor Davies (Ivor)	Bridgend
1955-1956	R. Bell (Dick)	Middlesborough
1956-1957	T. Price (Tommy)	Guildford
1957-1958	H.L. Parrack	Slough

1958-1959	H.E. Groves (Harry)	Bromley
1959-1960	J. Blackburn (Joe)	Pontefract
1960-1961	J. Ould (John)	Bermondsey
1961-1962	H. Brassington (Harry)	Nottingham
1962-1963	J. Cardwell (Jack)	Blackpool
1963-1964	A.V. Armstrong (Albert)	Wolverhampton
1964-1965	G.H. Morgan (George)	Bethnal Green
1965-1966	E.D. Evans (E.D.)	Swansea
1966-1967	A.W. Bullard (Alf)	Ipswich
1967	J. Sutherland (Jimmy)	Edinburgh
1967-1969	A.V. Uren (Alf)	Bow
1969-1970	W. Wass (Wilf)	Northallerton
1970-1971	A.R. Pinchin (Bob)	Croydon
1971-1972	W.G. Chatt (George)	Manchester
1972-1973	J. Barry (Jim)	Birkenhead
1973-1974	F.E. Lockley (Fred)	Exeter
1974-1975	E.J. Mew (John)	Isle of Wight
1975-1976	R.S. Reid (Bobby)	Aberdeen
1976-1977	F. West (Frank)	Lincolnshire
1977-1978	A. Yates (Alan)	Halifax
1978-1979	T.W. Griffiths (Tom)	Wolverhampton
1979-1980	T. Gunning (Tom)	Stevenage
1980-1981	P. Jones (Phil)	Birkenhead
1981-1982	P. Denning (Pat)	Merton
1982-1983	O. Davies (Olwen)	Neath
1983-1984	L. Stevens (Lil)	Birmingham
1984-1985	E.D. Davies (Dilwyn)	Leicester
1985-1986	E. Ward (Betty)	Oxford
1986-1987	J. Winsett (Joyce)	Barnsley
1987-1988	R. Baird (Ron)	Stockton
1988-1989	I. Love (Ina)	Glasgow
1989-1990	M. Page (Mike)	Leeds
1990-1991	W. Thorburn (Bill)	Edinburgh
1991-1992	J. Biggs (Jean)	Birmingham
1992-1993	A. McGonigle (Anna)	Omagh

Union Membership

1889	Municipal workers trade unionism begins
1894	6,000 (National Municipal Labour Union)
1906	16,000 (Municipal Employees Association)
1907	3,500 (National Union of Corporation Workers)
1928	12,500 (National Union of Public Employees)
1933	13,000
1937	33,000
1949	170,000
1958	200,000
1962	215,000
1968	256,000
1978	693,000
1982	710,000
1992	550,000